D1478515

Live Television

Live Television
The Golden Age of 1946–1958 in New York

by

Frank Sturcken

McFarland & Company, Inc., Publishers

Jefferson, North Carolina, and London

British Library Cataloguing-in-Publication data are available

Library of Congress Cataloguing-in-Publication Data

Sturcken, Frank, 1929–
    Live television : the golden age of 1946–1958 in New York / by
Frank Sturcken.
        p.   cm.
    [Includes index.]
    Includes bibliographical references.
    ISBN 0-89950-523-6 (lib. bdg. : 50# alk. paper) ∞
    1. Television plays, American—History and criticism.
    2. Television programs—United States.   I. Title.
    PN1992.3.U5S87   1990
    812'.02509054—dc20   89-43690
                                                          CIP

Manufactured in the United States of America

McFarland & Company, Inc., Publishers
    Box 611, Jefferson, North Carolina 28640

Acknowledgments

It is appropriate to thank the television professionals that provided original material for this book. Many of the most successful executives, producers and artists were willing to share—Pat Weaver, Hubbell Robinson, Jr., Albert McCleery, Worthington Miner, Rod Serling, Edmund Rice and many more. Much of this original material was collected between 1959 and 1963 and has been hoarded ever since. Eventually there was simply too much material to use.

I wish to express my particular gratitude to Jack Gould of *The New York Times*. He provided the best record of what happened in those years. Hal Humphry of *The Los Angeles Mirror* is not often quoted directly but his ideas are found throughout, as I was very much influenced by him and enjoyed his columns for many years in the early sixties.

I offer my special thanks to Pat Sturcken, Hal Algyer, Anne Sturcken and Dr. Arthur Ballet—to Pat and Anne for editing and typing, to Pat for her computer expertise, to Hal for editing and to Dr. Ballet for supervising the early research.

Table of Contents

Preface

This book is the inside story of the early days of television, of what happened in those years from 1946 to 1958, now often called the "Golden Years" of television. It focuses on the most significant programming feature of that time, *live* television. It is concerned with the people, the plays, and the performers. It marks television's growth from a strange gadget at the neighbor's house to an ordinary commodity and an ordinary part of our lives.

Was the live programming from 1946 to 1958 really quality programming? Did it flourish on television? Was it truly "golden" or just glitter? There is a kind of innocence surrounding the early days of television and we are curious to know if *live* television truly stood on its own feet, irrespective of its novelty aspects.

The great change in programming in 1958 came when the networks junked their production and programming plans, dropped New York, and went into partnership with the filmmakers. Eventually the quality of Hollywood television would go up, but what happened before then and why did the networks give up?

When media reporters and commentators of today refer to the Golden Age of television, they too frequently cite performers such as Jackie Gleason and shows such as *I Love Lucy*. They see filmed reruns. They forget, or just do not know, that the biggest and best of that period was all live from New York.

Only short years ago, Telstar brought television to an international threshold. Today cable has crossed the threshold into a large variety of programming. Pay television was another threshold that was promised to solve all the problems. It should be illuminating to visit that era of live network elegance in New York, which ended not by crossing a threshold, but by leaping off a cliff.

Over five years of searching out the facts in the memories of producers, directors, executives, the files of libraries and the archives of the television industry have revealed the story of a fascinating series of events unparalleled in the history of entertainment. On a single morning in that time, 65 million viewers could say, "I saw Mary Martin perform *live* last night," and, as Jack Gould, the critic of *The New York Times,* said, "Surely there must be a trace of fairy dust from coast to coast this morning."[1]

This book redresses my grievances. Many media writers and columnists are mistaken about early television. They write and talk about variety shows and film. Check the record herein. I have presented and documented something quite different.

1
Introduction

Remember . . .

The American television set has been around for over fifty years. It has served many functions, but none is more dominant than its role as storyteller. It all began in 1938 when NBC began broadcasting live television drama for the first time. There was a lull during World War II, then television finally emerged from the laboratory, bright with promise, glowing with expectations. *Kraft Theater, Studio One,* and *Philco Playhouse* opened for business. *Playhouse 90* and *Hallmark Hall of Fame* followed. Playwrights from Shakespeare and Shaw to Pushkin and Pirandello, Serling and Chayefsky to Wilde and Wharton, gave that early television in New York some elegance and distinction. Over 5,000 dramas in a new form with a new emphasis were broadcast live to the largest audiences in history. By any standards, this was storytelling of some consequence.

The problem of feeding the hungry electronic beast has been the overworked metaphor concerning television production. Young producers such as Fred Coe, Albert McCleery, and Worthington Miner, and young executives such as Pat Weaver and Hubbell Robinson, Jr., fed the hungry beast exceptional originals such as *Patterns* and *Marty.* They borrowed stories from the stage, *Peter Pan, Mr. Roberts, Our Town.* They revived classics, *Hamlet, Macbeth, She Stoops to Conquer.* "Howdy Doody" became a household word. Ed Sullivan was host of the *Toast of the Town* and Edward R. Murrow appeared with his cigarette—all live from New York.

Live drama in the hour-long series variety became television's most

1

exceptional form in those early days. In spite of the fact that those series were the pace-setters in terms of quality, for many years live drama withstood the flood of mysteries, situation comedies and quiz shows; it maintained a large audience, and a satisfying sales report for the sponsor. Live television at its best achieved great dramatic production and distinguished original playwriting. At its worst it was hasty and one-dimensional and previewed the "soaps" of today's daytime television.

There were workers and dreamers such as NBC executive Pat Weaver, and play producer Fred Coe, who visualized this medium as engendering a new kind of drama, a complete departure from the often shoddy, repetitious programming of radio, and the slick, cheap films of Hollywood.

"Lordy, it was exciting," said television critic John Crosby. "It was wild" said Hubbell Robinson, Jr., formerly a CBS vice president. "We shall create the Great American Theater" said Pat Weaver. New actors, directors and playwrights were being discovered by the dozens. Champagne flowed, and the great (dramatic) American Dream was no longer Hollywood's or Broadway's, it was television's. Good or bad, by 1955–56 there were as many as 16 live stories broadcast nationally every week.

Early in the game, the movie moguls had taken a hasty look over their shoulders and decided to ignore this brash new thing. And who needed the motion picture industry? Every time one opened the papers one could read that NBC was adding a new color studio or CBS was opening a Television City.

And Then Crash . . .

During the 1955–56 television season, industry personnel were predicting that live two-hour dramas as a regular feature and in a regular series format were just around the corner. Yet another end was already in sight. No one dreamed that in the following two short years the filmed Western would do what Milton Berle and the filmed situation comedies had failed to do. What was heralded as a great revolution in the American theatrical arts amounted to rather "small change" as television moved to Hollywood and the "B" movie makers moved from the corner popcorn house to the living room.

The huge television studio production plants that the networks had built became empty tombs. A few ghosts loitered around in the crypts for a while: soap operas and live news and game shows, but all of the "live ones" have long ago departed.

Most of the top, the best, the most talented producers, directors and writers quickly and successfully moved on to Broadway and to Hollywood. The live television industry was a fertile training ground for the talents behind the scenes. Their names are generally unfamiliar: Fred Coe began producing; Arthur Penn was directing; Vincent Donahue did *Sunrise at Campobello;* John Frankenheimer and Rod Serling began making films; Chayefsky and Mosel had hits on Broadway. There were many, many more. It was sad when they left. The promise of shows such as *Kraft Television Theater, Philco Playhouse, Producer's Showcase, Studio One,* and *Playhouse 90* was broken by the network programming from 1958 to the mid-1960's. That period had the dreariest pretence at dramatic entertainment that any medium had ever perpetrated upon an audience.

The eminent television critic, John Crosby, abdicated in 1960 with a self proclaimed "swan song":

> Television no longer deserves daily criticism on a serious level.... Silence is the only sensible greeting for "Pete and Gladys," "Hong Kong," "Argonauts," and the rest of the dreary new shows.... Television isn't awful. Awful things are fun to write about. If it were bad enough, we critics could denounce it. But "Rawhide" isn't really that awful. It's a bore.[1]

The hue and cry ranged the length of the land. And it was not just the high culture buffs railing at a mass culture success story. The Federal Communications Commission (FCC), the United States Senate, the eggheads, certainly, but also a number of just plain folks seemed genuinely appalled at the quick and drastic change in programming and the seeming dedication to vacuity. "It's not true," said NBC chairman Robert Sarnoff as he cited new programming ventures, "that this season's (any season from 1958 to 1964) programming is a rehash of previous years'."[2]

In the ensuing years television became one of the major whipping boys for the American public, second only to the Russians and the public schools as a source of all of their troubles. Maybe the new baby had simply lost its bloom, but a great many people in those days were genuinely concerned. The apologists of those years have explained that

Westerns and mysteries were all the public wanted. The fact is, there has never been any great public disenchantment with television. Perhaps television has lost some of the initial allure for the public, and perhaps sometimes people turn on their television sets when they have nothing else to do. Certainly people do not talk about last night's television show as much as they used to. In any case the novelty wore off and the criticism began. In many homes watching television became a synonym for taking a cat nap. The criticism grew and the networks stirred around and it all built to FCC chairman Newton Minow's famous statement that television is a "vast wasteland."

"We're steeped in nostalgia," said Hubbell Robinson, Jr., a former executive at CBS. "Much that we did seems better than it was." Then he warmed up to his topic. "But we did do some good and great things." And he finally admitted when consulted in 1961, "It has declined terribly. It's a mess of pottage. I find it hard to look at, but I'm getting a chance to read again."[3] Pat Weaver, a former executive at NBC, was quite frank when interviewed in 1959. "It stinks. The audience is running away. The nets buy junk in cans from 'B' movie people and pretend they're program people."[4]

Dr. Frank Stanton, president of CBS, and Leonard H. Goldenson, head of ABC, indicated little concern at that time about the quality of television. They frankly admitted their goals as lowest common denominator programming. Dr. Stanton testified at a United States Senate hearing,

> If I am correct in my definition of the basic nature of television, we must face the fact that it is a major part of our function to try to appeal to most of the people most of the time. . . . It is not an elite medium. . . . We cannot force people to like what they don't like, to want what they don't want.[5]

Goldenson of ABC was direct: "These minority groups—these eggheads—are not big TV watchers anyway. Television is a mass medium, and we don't want to lose this status."[6]

The two ex-executives, Robinson and Weaver, were program people. Robinson explained, "There are no creative men in the networks today. They're all businessmen, buying and selling." After resigning, Weaver had his say: "The networks cannot do their job because of inter-network warfare based on program ratings and high costs." The firing or resignation of creative executives such as Weaver and Robinson were obviously symptoms, not causes.

The general public is inclined to think of the television networks as the shows' producers. This is far from true. And the question of "who produces what?" is only part of the answer. The varied relationships among the networks, the advertising and talent agencies, the independent television producers, and the film industry are vastly complicated. In telling the story of live television, it is difficult to determine what forces were responsible for what. In the early stages of the game the networks did attempt to dominate programming and competed with many outside sources of talent and materials for production profit. The William Morris Agency and the Music Corporation of America, for example, controlled enough talent in the country to deny the networks the "name" stars; therefore they produce for themselves or support independent operations.[7]

Under the trade name Revere Productions, MCA, known to the trade as the "Octopus," eventually became one of the biggest and most successful of all television packagers. Its television policy was to produce television shows that would sell, based on the "follow the leader" psychology prevalent in Hollywood. The William Morris Agency did not produce shows but it was the exclusive selling agent for one of the largest packagers in those days, Four Star Productions. In the beginning, they and MCA concentrated on inexpensive situation comedies. Showcase Productions and Talent Associates are examples of the independent package producers in the field of drama. One advertising agency, J. Walter Thompson, was eminently successful producing shows such as *Kraft Television Theater* and *Lux Video Theater*.

One thing does seem apparent. In the early days the networks seemed to maintain varying degrees of programming control. They developed programs with their own organizations, financed others, farmed others out or worked jointly with independents.[8] This is an oversimplified answer to the question of "who produced what" on television up to 1958. There is no clear-cut picture. The fact remains that the networks exercised some creative control and maintained large creative staffs to investigate shows, produce them, or obtain them from the outside.

It is also clear that the networks dismissed their creative staffs when the programming moved to Hollywood. Film studios and independent filmmakers began to produce the majority of television dramas and sold them, not to networks, but to advertisers. And the networks? They began to provide the mechanical service of beaming these films through

the lines that they rented from AT&T. The networks occasionally produced films for television, however, and the filmmakers often cut the
networks into their production pie, mostly in the areas of planning and
profit.

Filmed drama in the beginning of television's sojourn in Hollywood was simply motion pictures made for television and was a product
of the Hollywood motion picture industry. In contrast, the production
of live or taped television directly involved the television industry. The
type of live television associated with the beginnings of television
broadcasting came from New York in a unified performance in which
the action was continuous and, in the case of drama and variety shows,
it was seen by an audience as it was performed. In this respect, the live
television drama was close to the stage play; its peculiar characteristic
was its immediacy. In a second respect, live television was close to the
motion picture. Each views the subject through the lens of a camera.

The Prewar Experimental Programs

In 1928 *The New York Times* carried a front page headline: "Play
Is Broadcast By Voice And Acting In Radio-Television." This first
transmission of a dramatic performance on television was accomplished
by the General Electric research laboratory through its pioneer station,
WGY at Schenectady, New York. To publicize their engineering accomplishments GE chose a forty-minute broadcast of an old spy
melodrama, *The Queen's Messenger* by J. Hartley Manners. The *Times*
stated that this play was chosen because "its cast contains only two actors who could alternate before the three cameras and a microphone."
"While the actors went through their parts in a locked studio room their
appearances and voices" were carried by wire to a transmitting station
four miles away; there they were broadcast and picked up at the place
of origin.[9] An early work by Orrin Dunlap, published in 1932, has some
rare pictures of this production revealing the crudeness of equipment
and settings.[10]

Some researcher erred and the television files of the New York
Public Library erroneously list an obscure extravaganza called *The
Mysterious Mummy Case* as the first television drama, and the date as
1938. That is just ten years behind the institution of the era of television
by the broadcast of a television drama.

Television, like radio, had its beginnings in the nineteenth century. Not only were the scientific foundations laid, but numerous attempts were made to transmit pictures by electrical means. It was not until the electronic cathode ray tube was developed about 1915 that it was possible to produce a television picture of decent quality and individuals began to think about commercial television.[11] The cathode ray tube made it feasible by converting the intensities of the light rays from the image to be televised into electronic impulses which could be transmitted over wire and through the air.

In 1923 Dr. V.K. Zworkin had patented an electronic pick-up tube, the iconoscope tube that had relatively good picture quality, but required extremely strong light for effectiveness.[12] The tube went through various stages of development and by the 1930's television had reached a fairly high stage of technical development.[13] With the major technical problems solved, it was in 1938 that broadcasters first began to study production methods and operational procedures in attempts to bring order and efficiency to the many complex components that make up a television broadcast. By 1938 there were 18 stations in the United States licensed to broadcast on an experimental basis.[14]

The first actual major telecast was staged on April 7, 1927, by AT&T. It was a speech by Herbert Hoover as Secretary of Commerce that was telecast by wire from Washington to New York. The immortal first words were those of an AT&T vice president, "I am instructed to make a little conversation while they are getting the loudspeakers ready." The *Times* headline read, "Far Off Speaker Seen As Well As Heard ... Like A Photo Come To Life" and while the *Times* subheadline indicated "Commercial Use in Doubt," the event was prophetic: "next was a vaudeville act ... a stage Irishman."[15]

In the thirties, everyone's chief concern was with pick-up tubes and picture quality. There was one entrepreneur, however, whose imagination was fired beyond the immediate technical problems into a consideration of television's production problems and its artistic future. This gentleman, David Sarnoff, was to become television's foremost champion. Years before, in 1916, when he was a 25-year-old assistant traffic manager for Marconi, the inventor of wireless radio, he wrote a memo that set the pattern for radio and eventually for television:

I have in mind a plan of development which would make a radio a household utility in the same sense as the piano or the phonograph. The idea is to bring music into the home by wireless. The same principle can be extended to numerous other fields, as, for example, receiving lectures at home, which can be simultaneously announced and received. Baseball scores could be transmitted in the air.[16]

In an amazing address, "Radio-Vision Era Is Dawning," at the early date of 1931, David Sarnoff was charting television's course and keenly predicting its future. On the front page of *The New York Times* he predicted:

It [television] will prove a welcome stimulant, a pleasant tonic to all the entertaining arts..., furnishing a new and greater outlet for artistic expression.... Special types of distribution networks, new forms of stagecraft and a development of studio equipment and techniques will be required.

New forms of artistry will be encouraged and developed. Variety and more variety will be the demand of the day. The ear might be content with the oft-repeated song; the eye would be impatient with the twice-repeated scene. The service will demand: a constant succession of personalities, a vast array of talent, a tremendous store of material, a great variety of scene and background.[17]

The Formal Debut

"TV Is Just Around The Corner..." Television made its formal debut in April of 1939 when NBC broadcast President Roosevelt's speech at the opening of the New York World's Fair.[18] That same day RCA put its first receiving sets on sale with prices ranging from $199.50 for the smallest to $600 for the 10" by 12" size. Because of the wide publicity Gertrude Lawrence received in the play *Susan and God,* the "official" inauguration of drama came the year before, however.

The tragic loss of the early television shows because there was not yet a method of recording them was in a small way rectified by *Life* magazine, which preserved an historical record of what the television camera caught in the *Susan and God* production in a series of ten photographs of a television receiver. *Life*'s pictures are remarkably clear and well-defined.[19] This, of course, was the whole point. It was obviously the most essential value in a broadcast in those days—"Could you *really* see it?" *Life* commented, "the images were lucid and sharply defined" and the lead-off statement in *The New York Times* review is quite revealing: "The scenes were *clearly* televised." The reviewer found "the scenery and costumes were exactly as seen on the stage" and was pleased that "the viewing's perfect, no audience's heads to dodge, no latecomers to disturb the continuity."[20]

With David Sarnoff's unending interest in the new medium and with the financial resources of RCA, it was natural that NBC should take the leading role in projecting television into a big time operation, and the leading role in making drama its number one format. In 1938 NBC's flagship station, W2XBS (later WNBC), began to broadcast experimentally from atop the Empire State Building in a bid for public interest. At the start there were three afternoon transmissions of test charts and still pictures and two evening programs of entertainment each week.[21]

It was apparent to NBC's staff, headed by Thomas Hutchinson, that storytelling was eminently suited to the new medium. Television adaptations of popular Broadway shows were presented as the Wednesday night feature of these broadcasts. Among the offerings were *Jane Eyre, Susan and God, Brother Rat,* and *June Moon.*[22]

One of the earliest of these productions was the aforementioned *The Mysterious Mummy Case.* It was, at the time, generally applauded as the "most professional" to date, for "sixteen hours of rehearsal were required to polish the performance."[23] Hutchinson wrote about NBC's work and commented that these first dramas were simple, short scenes, but "as the success of this entertainment was proved, the plays presented became longer, the casts larger, and the productions more pretentious."[24]

Under the impetus of this regular dramatic fare, *The New York Times* ran its first conventional review of a "teleplay" in a column "Televiews of Pictures" by Orrin Dunlap. The production was *Dulcy* by Kaufman and Connelly, and Dunlap commented that as an amusing telecast "it proved beyond all doubt that drama is one of TV's aces." In this column, which was to become a weekly feature, Dunlap complained prophetically in his first review, "the difficulty here is, however, that the show despite its long rehearsal is gone in one showing. There is no second night!"[25]

It should also be noted that the Columbia Broadcasting System also began serious experimentation in 1937, when space was leased in the Grand Central Terminal and Gilbert Seldes was engaged as manager of program development. By 1939 equipment was installed and closed circuit telecasts were made. Broadcasts did not begin until 1941 because of delay in installing the aerial on the Chrysler Building,[26] and because the FCC ordered a halt in television expansion in 1940 until the best standards for transmission could be determined.[27] When CBS finally began a program service of 15 hours a week in 1941 they had to cease operation the next year because of the war, and they did not broadcast again until 1944 when the Grand Central studios were reopened and a new staff assembled.[28]

World War II

In 1941, six months before the United States entered World War II, the FCC rescinded its order of 1940 that had halted television's development and once again authorized full commercial television on the black and white standard still in use.[29] NBC had the only station prepared to accommodate advertisers and was granted the first commercial license under the name WNBT.[30] Television was off and running. World War II was just around the corner and the situation quickly changed, but it looked good for a while. NBC got its rate cards out, listing a full hour of television in the prime evening time as costing sponsors $120![31] It is now routine to pay $100,000 or more for a 30-second commercial on *Miami Vice* or *Dallas*.

The FCC accommodated those stations wishing to hold onto their licenses during the war by reducing the minimum broadcast time from 15 hours a week to four. Five stations across the country kept television alive during the war through their attempts to meet these requirements. The New York stations WNBT and DuMont were limited in their programming to films with an occasional instructional program for civilian defense.[32]

Television was crippled by the war effort just as it had begun to look promising. Many speculated about "the thirty million dollar if," that being approximately the amount spent developing television up to the war.[33] One writer in the *Saturday Review*, who withheld his name, went so far as to suggest in 1942 that television was not so much a "war casualty" as a victim of "the powerful interests in the press, the movies and the radio" who "put it as far back on the shelf as they could because they saw in it a threat to their status quo."[34] Gilbert Seldes of

CBS answered the critic with the comment, "Your critic says that we are being held back. I assure you we have our hands full."[35]

Television was ready to explode. NBC had pioneered commercial television service in the United States and the production of drama as part of that service. It was immediately apparent to NBC's staff headed by Thomas Hutchinson, and later the CBS and DuMont units, that drama was eminently suited to the new medium. In New York, where television programming got its start, drama was a ready-made form of entertainment. George Norford, director of information at NBC, suggested when remembering those days that the producers "were trained in the legitimate theater.... We had no money and quiet little intimate dramas were easy to produce."[36]

Television drama in its brief live existence must be considered a unique form developed by and for networks of stations to meet the prime time broadcast needs of the new industry. As it grew it borrowed staging techniques from the theater, camera techniques from motion pictures, broadcasting techniques from radio, and, some think, quickly imposed on them all its own unique forms.

2
The Age of Television Begins

The True Age Dawns, Finally

It was not until August 14, 1945, that Japan surrendered, yet interest in postwar television had begun building since as early as 1944. By June of that year there were 52 applications for station licenses on file with the FCC. By April of 1946 there were 144.[1] Though programming had come to a standstill during the war years, engineering and technical advances had continued, improving picture quality and thus entertainment potential. The problem of program expense would, it was thought, be solved by the development of networks through intercity cables and, most importantly, American production methods would bring the price of television sets within the range of everyone. Television was on the move and by April of 1946 seven commercial stations were operating in the United States: three in New York and one each in Chicago, Schenectady, Philadelphia, and Washington.

In March 1944, NBC had announced its plans for a national television network, with a regional Eastern network as the first step. This announcement came simultaneously with station WNBT's first network broadcast to Philadelphia and Schenectady.[2] Previously, the American Telephone and Telegraph Company had announced its intentions of laying coaxial cable designed to carry the television signal between the major cities throughout the United States — a very costly and time consuming operation.[3] The aim was to completely network the country. The alternative to the use of coaxial cable was kinescoped film, or kinescopes as they came to be called. The poor quality of the reproduced picture was a serious defect of kinescopes.

13

The growth of networks was an inevitable phenomenon. As previously mentioned the idea was similar to the radio networks already in operation. A major difference between radio and television, however, was the great cost of television programming, even on a local basis. It was clear that because of tremendous expenses a single program would need a large audience to be commercially feasible.

It is significant to note that Zenith Radio Corporation had already laid plans as early as 1945 for subscription television! Having patented a "scrambling" device, Zenith proposed this as the only practical method of financing programming.[4] It is interesting to speculate on the course television would have taken had Zenith obtained Federal approval of its pay television approach. Zenith had bigger problems than the FCC, however. Zenith's failure to develop pay television lay in the nature and size of its two major opponents: AT&T and RCA!

Major Obstacles to Growth

Program expense was only the first of television's problems. At the outset, a quick national growth might have been expected. There were, however, considerable delays. Television had lost public interest in the rush production of luxury goods following the war, and for a number of years after the war, people were more concerned with refrigerators and cars than they were with squinting at bad shows on the little picture tube. David Sarnoff of NBC was, as always, a prophet and proponent of the electrical revolution. But he admitted that NBC and the industry had "oversold" the public before the war and had not made good on their promise.[5]

Whereas early prewar efforts were carefully chronicled, the New York papers rarely mentioned postwar television except to list program schedules. Jack Gould, *The New York Times* radio columnist, and John Crosby, of the *New York Herald Tribune*, seldom discussed television until 1949. The leading trade magazine, *Broadcasting*, did not concern itself with television except to list the activities of the FCC. It changed its name to *Broadcasting-Telecasting* in 1950, perhaps inadvertently implying that telecasting is not broadcasting. It went back to the single name a few years later. Americans were simply more concerned with new cars after the war than they were with watching television shows of dubious value.

A second major problem was the controversy that developed over which band television should be assigned in the broadcast spectrum and whether transmission should be in black-and-white or color. A prolonged color controversy between CBS and the colossus, NBC, was heightened in November of 1946 by an announcement from NBC that it had achieved color electronically, as opposed to CBS's mechanical system. Finally, after 14 weeks of testimony, the FCC ruled out color for the immediate future and authorized black-and-white television over 13 channels in the very high frequency, or VHF range. Within six months the number of applications for television stations jumped to more than 300.[6]

Television's third problem was its biggest problem, and is its eternal problem. How do you fill up that rectangular space day in and day out, 52 weeks a year? Although there were many applicants for television stations and many acquired construction permits, the "28 hour rule" of the FCC, requiring 28 hours of programming a week, went into effect June 20, 1946. It resulted in many withdrawn applications and relinquished construction permits.[7]

The telecasters had full schedules to maintain and little money. They desperately needed program material and they begged the movie companies to release to them, rent, sell, or give, any kind of old films which they could televise to take up space between the few studio shows and special events available. Generally the movie companies were uncooperative on the grounds that the telecasting of films would empty theatres.[8]

This was the normal neurotic condition of Hollywood. When radio and talking pictures came along Hollywood had also tried to delay or prevent their growth for fear they would kill the industry. Now it was television, and later it would be Pat Weaver's subscription television on cable.[9] Television producer Albert McCleery gave his vivid opinion to this writer at a later date: "the Movie Moguls turned their backs, knelt down facing west, and prayed it would go away!"[10] It would be a long time before the correct formula was worked out for celluloid's marriage with the new medium.

Philip Gustafson, a management consultant, looked at television in 1947 and commented in the magazine *Nation's Business:* "Program wise, television suffers from growing pains that would kill anything but a hardened war-waif bred in starvation." Television programming was suffering from a lack of space, shortages of equipment, and a scarcity

of trained personnel. Mr. Gustafson concluded that the baby's environ-
ment was unhealthy because it had "a backwoods full of feuds" pro-
voked by the rivals CBS and NBC.[11]

Those stations on the air, however, had to provide service. It is
generally agreed that the programs were inferior—an endless succession
of wrestling matches, roller-skating derbys, parlor games, animal acts,
and sporting events. Television had progressed beyond the point where
the audiences' major concern was "was it a good picture?" It was very
difficult to do a bad show, however, because television's novelty was
such a useful asset. So great was the medium's power to enchant people
that the mere act of placing something, anything, on the screen was
enough to guarantee an audience—for a while.[12]

When they were bored with Benny and Hope on radio, the critics
would occasionally look at television and comment on the serious deficiencies of video art.[13] Producer Albert McCleery of the *Hallmark Hall
of Fame* show and Edmund Rice of *Kraft Theater* emphasized when interviewed how much could be "gotten away with" at this stage of the
game. If the quality level of video programming was as depressing as
it was pictured then what would happen when the novelty wore off?
Something had to be done and fast. After all, RCA had television sets
to sell!

NBC Pioneers Television Drama

It was NBC, through its New York station WNBT, that made
preparations to remedy the program deficiencies outlined above.
Through its parent RCA, NBC had the financial resources that the
other stations lacked. It thus gets full credit for projecting television
into a big time operation by taking the leading role in making drama
its number one prime time offering.

Storytelling had been big in radio and it received a major share of
the attention in postwar television planning. The legitimate theatre
scripts were written; the legitimate theatre actors and directors were
trained; and the programming void needed filling. So WNBC executives set out to build a staff capable of producing, directing and design-
ing plays.

In April of 1945 John Royal, executive director at WNBT, hired
theatre-trained Fred Coe as a production assistant. Coe was one of the

earliest of many Yale-trained drama graduates who would come to network television. "Mr. Television Drama" had left his job at a little theatre in Columbia, South Carolina, and had been hanging around New York looking for television work. He had given up and was preparing to leave town when Mr. Royal called him. Within a month Coe directed his first play for a late afternoon children's show.[14]

The career of one of live television's finest producer-directors was launched with a television version of DeMaupassant's *The Necklace*. In the years to come this man would be closely identified with live television's greatest triumphs: productions such as *Marty, Peter Pan,* and *Other People's Houses;* and dramatic series such as *Philco Television Playhouse, Producer's Showcase,* and *Playhouse 90.*[15]

Fred Coe directed many of the monthly Sunday evening dramas in the 1946–47 season under the heading *Television Theatre*. Full length, three-act plays became known as WNBT's "Sunday Night Forte." Towards the end of that season the Borden Company picked up the sponsorship of these shows with a production of *Twelfth Night* and carried it through one production in the fall.[16] The Shakespearean comedy was done in a 70-minute version with Borden's commercial confined to the opening and closing spots. Borden's temporary support of *Television Theatre* gains it the honor of being the first sponsor of Sunday night dramas on NBC, a dignified sponsorship also held later with great honor and financial success by the Philco, Goodyear, and Alcoa Aluminum companies. Several New York reviewers described the show as "top drawer entertainment" and "good Shakespeare."[17]

Kraft Television Theater

The most significant event of the 1946–47 season, and maybe of network television's first ten years, occurred on May 7, 1947. *Kraft Television Theater* opened as the first weekly hour-long dramatic series on the new medium. Sunday night *Television Theatre* had been an on and off affair in contrast to the regularity of *Kraft's* broadcasts. Kraft was to have the longest run of any of the successful live dramatic series that were to follow and the longest run of anything since. Incredibly, it missed only three live telecasts in eleven and a half years, including summers, and then only because its time on the air was preempted by presidential conventions. Throughout its distinguished history *Kraft* was to be selected by NBC to achieve other television firsts: it was the first show to be televised over the Midwest coaxial cable and was the first dramatic show to be televised in compatible color.[18]

The *Kraft* idea came about not from the Sunday *Television Theatre* but from a show produced by the J. Walter Thompson advertising agency called *The Hour Glass Show*. In May of 1946 J. Walter Thompson suggested to one of its clients, Standard Brands, that it experiment with the new medium in advertising Chase and Sanborn coffee. The *Hour Glass* program resulted and it followed the pattern of a variety show in which most productions contained a short one-act play or skit. These one-act plays were quite popular with the Thompson staff and they received considerable audience mail. Among the plays Edmund Rice edited for these spots were *Farewell Supper* by Arthur Schnitzler, *The Jest of Hahalaba* by Lord Dunsany, and *A Tooth for Paul Revere* by Steven Vincent Benét.[19]

After spending two and a half million dollars Standard Brands asked to be released. The company had not expected advertising value per dollar and felt it "had acquired enough experimentation to wait for a larger audience." The J. Walter Thompson company, however, thought it could do for television what it had done for radio with *Lux Radio Theater*. Because of the simplicity of production it had been quite common in radio for advertising agencies to produce shows and then sell them to advertisers. Edmund Rice of the Thompson staff remembered specifically what had happened:

> After a couple of hours of the *Hour Glass* show we began to believe drama would go well on television. John Reber—who is now dead—was in charge of television at J. Walter Thompson and he was strong for television drama. I prepared a presentation and then we sold it to Kraft. If we had to give a title, John Reber would be our Executive Producer. Stanley Quinn directed every show and I wrote every show for a long, long time.[20]

Kraft liked Rice's presentation, signed a one year contract with NBC, and *Double Door* opened on May 7. Because so few people were trained in the technical operation of a television studio, the early NBC production format required one of its own directors, in this case Fred Coe, to take over when the play reached the studios.

This historically important first production was housed in a tiny studio on a side corridor in Radio City and broadcast to an audience of less than 40,000, for there were only slightly more than 43,000 sets in the nation at that time. The play had had a long run on Broadway in 1933 but the television critics were unhappy with it. *"Kraft* got off to a faulty start," said *Variety,* "through the unfortunate selection of a dull, overly-done melodrama that has lost whatever merit it might have once possessed through the passage of time."[21] But the show was carefully and smoothly produced and *Kraft* was pleased. It was on this very first show that producer Quinn introduced the famous trademark of the series, the large-blocked "K" and the accompanying toy-sized cameraman.

Many of the early *Kraft* shows bombed with the critics.[22] But the audience was intrigued and the Kraft Company was delighted. On the first few shows it was decided to test the effectiveness of the new medium by advertising a new product, MacLaren's Imperial Cheese. It was the only product advertised, and it was only advertised in live commercials on television.[23] "It was sensationally successful," said Rice, "with only a few thousand sets." The vivid nature of television advertising was nowhere more successfully demonstrated than when the camera dollied in onto the slicing of several thick pieces of MacLaren's Imperial Cheese. In addition, *Kraft* had been having trouble with a new product, presliced processed cheese. Fewer housewives wrote in and complained after the young actress demonstrated how to peel the slices off.

Kraft Television Theater quickly came to assume a personality of its own. This resulted from the goals of the J. Walter Thompson presentation, their elaborations as the show continued, and the show's low budget in contrast to other series. Although little publicized and seldom reviewed in the many years that followed, *Kraft* became a pleasant habit to the television audience, and was consistently in the top ten of the audience surveys. This caused some concern among the sponsors of the other early-hour dramas, none of which made it to the top ten in their first seasons, with budgets four times as large as *Kraft's.* The *Kraft Television Theater* was an amazing feat for an advertising agency. The much-maligned advertising business can look with pride at J. Walter Thompson's accomplishment. In fact, the much-maligned advertising business can look with great pride at the many television firsts that were inspired by this company.

The J. Walter Thompson company was the first to produce a full variety show on television for Shell — in 1940 — and the first to telecast a baseball World Series, for Ford in 1947. There were many more firsts

for this adventurous advertising agency—the first rodeo and horse
shows in 1946, the first to bring the World Series out of town back to
New York—and in 1949 they had five sponsored shows in one evening.
(They also produced the first dog show and if horse shows were an accomplishment in those days, one can imagine the problems they had
with the dogs.)[24]

But it was *Kraft Theater* that was the most significant of their firsts.
Those many Americans who had an 11-year love affair with *Kraft*,
despite the over-eating that was stimulated by their commercials, will
understand Rice's description of their policies in the 1950 edition of
Best Television Plays:

> Our aims in the very beginning were to build in our audience the habit
> of tuning into Kraft. The actors were not top stars and the play was
> usually unfamiliar, so we attempted to get our audience to *expect a*
> *good story.*[25]

Maury Holland, a *Kraft* producer, also stated in the same volume:

> We feel that we have a steady family audience that tunes into the *Kraft*
> *Television Theater* every Wednesday evening with the assurance that
> they're going to see a good play. Judging by the mail that has come,
> our viewers have come to look upon the show much in the manner of
> the theater-goer who buys a season ticket because he has found by ex-
> perience that week in and week out he will see a good drama.[26]

The 1947–48 Season

This was the season that television went big time. Howdy Doody
and Milton Berle joined *Kraft Television Theater* and sports programming began to come into its own. Sports occupied the number one spot
in the programming for several seasons and sold enough TV sets to keep
RCA investors happy. The set manufacturers had begun to hit their
stride and they were selling all the sets they could make. As the audience size increased that season, some television stations increased
their fees as much as 50 percent.

The race was also on for networks and station licenses. KSTP-TV
of Minneapolis signed the first station affiliation contract with NBC, in
March of 1948, and in the same month received program service by a
film technique called kinescopes.[27] It was quickly followed by stations

in Richmond and Cincinnati, and in the following week nine more had signed contracts with NBC.[28] CBS signed Baltimore at the end of March and in the following week signed eight more affiliates.[29] The rush for station licenses in the East began to spread steadily westward. There was a shortage of spectrum space in contrast to demand, and the FCC was having "the devil of a time" trying to secure an orderly yet rapid growth.[30] But General Sarnoff was feeling better about it and once again was making predictions. He was a little premature in describing television as "a major social, economic and artistic force," but the stations on the air were expanding schedules and by July 1948 thirty were broadcasting and had greatly expanded schedules.[31]

In those years sports constituted an entertainment that was ready-made in proven entertainment value. The first televising of the World Series and the broadcast of the Louis-Walcott boxing match from Madison Square Garden made the picture box quite popular. *Variety* reported after the world series that "Broadway box office suffered a fifty percent slump with matinees kayoed, but bars with television upped 500 percent."[32] This was the season of Henny Youngman's famous gag: "Bartender wanted; must be able to fix TV set." And television was described the following summer as the "wonder of the year" when it covered the national Republican and Democratic conventions in Philadelphia.[33] Ben Cross of the *Daily News* gave a vivid picture of the unusual developments in Manhattan in his book, *I Looked and I Listened:*

> Families borrowed and scrimped to buy television sets; soon friends and casual acquaintances crowded the living rooms to gaze at Milton Berle; beds were unmade and soiled dishes filled the sinks; school kids ignored the homework; taverns displayed signs, "FREE TV TONIGHT."[34]

As Edmund Rice of *Kraft Theater* pictured drama programs, they were "no small timers" in comparison. Broadway got into the act and the high and mighty Theatre Guild and the American National Theatre and Academy lent respectability and professionalism in their attempts at series drama. The Theatre Guild made arrangements with NBC in October of 1947 for joint presentation of a series of six plays on television. *John Ferguson* by St. John Ervine had been the Theatre Guild's first major success in 1919, and was chosen as the premier production with Thomas Mitchell as the star and Edward Sobel as the producer.[35] It was transmitted on a four-city network, recorded on film and

sent to NBC affiliates in Detroit and St. Louis. There was no sponsor
but NBC paid heavily for the best in talent and production. It was a
highly publicized venture and as a result was a major step in the
development of television drama. The Theater Guild stated its purpose
was to build television into "a straw hatter for the showing of new plays
and talent."[36]

The reviews were unfavorable and few individuals today
remember the series. *Variety* was polite as it stated that the Guild made
"a promising but unfortunate entry into television." The reviewer,
Stahl, describes the script as "decrepit," resembling a remake of *The
Drunkard*.[37] Jack Gould of the *Times* was not so kind, charging that
the Guild ventured out in the strange world of television and "promptly
fell on its art." He criticized the Guild for allowing sentiment to influence the choice of production, stating the play was the "grand-daddy
of the soap opera writers." It is true that the play has a mortgaged
homestead, a villain, a ravished daughter, and a brother who avenged
her honor. To the television audience these incidents were thrown in
an excessively melodramatic frame. Gould explained that in cutting the
script NBC settled for the narrative, or bare plot, leaving the characterizations weak.[38]

After six productions, the Guild contracted with NBC to produce
another six dramas but a sponsor could not be found. Several sponsors
were reportedly ready to pay $12,000 every week but the Guild felt that
with its many interests it could not do justice to more than one show
a month.[39] The sponsors were still thinking in terms of radio with its
regular weekly broadcasts. There was also a feeling at that time that
advertisers would never be able to afford thousands of dollars for a
single showing of any lengthy or complicated production because the
value would be nil after one nationwide showing. NBC had grander
plans; it continued to spend money and its productions grew in
lavishness and dimension. For NBC the gamble would begin to pay off
in a few seasons. For the Theatre Guild, it would eventually pay off with
the lengthy and successful run of the *U.S. Steel Hour*.

The American National Theatre and Academy (ANTA) was not
quite so fortunate. ANTA and NBC planned a series of half hour
dramas in the fall of the 1947–48 season. For the second time in that
season NBC was looking to Broadway theatrical producers when it
wanted to broadcast drama. Their first production was Tennessee
Williams' *The Last of My Solid Gold Watches*. Twenty-four hours

before the first broadcast on December 4, 1947, *A Streetcar Named Desire* had opened and the New York critics were doing handsprings over Tennessee Williams. This excited some interest in the ANTA television opening that was originally scheduled before *Streetcar's* Broadway opening but was "fortunately" postponed because of "technical difficulties."[40] The story of the old salesman and his "solid gold watches," living on past glories and unwilling to accept the changing world, was ironically and prophetically similar to ANTA's and the Theatre Guild's views of television.

The ANTA series also could be said to have died when no sponsor could be found. It was not the last of the many attempts to "bring Broadway to all of America," but it marked the end of that period when television was regarded as simply the opportunity to photograph a play.

The Big Freeze

A television signal is a roadhog on the airways. It requires 600 times the width of the path required by a radio signal and signals on the same path interfere so badly with one another that they must be clearly separated. In September 1948 the FCC, hearing the effects of signal interference as more and more stations took to the air, imposed a freeze on the processing of station applications. The 70 station applicants who had received permits prior to that date were permitted to proceed with the construction of their stations.

For the three and a half years of this famous big freeze the Commission investigated the best frequency allocation plan, and what policy the FCC should adopt for color.[41] For three and a half years the 106 operating and licensed stations had time to entrench their positions with no fears of immediate new competition. In these years television sets began to be mass produced. Movie attendance began to fall in cities with television stations and by 1960 in New York alone 50 movie theaters would close their doors forever. If television went big time in 1947–48, then television drama went big time in 1948–49 with *Philco Playhouse, Ford Theater,* and *Studio One.*

The main problem for the independent stations in 1948 was still financial. No single network and very few stations were yet showing a profit, with operating costs already five times more expensive than radio. As the year closed, however, nearly 900,000 television sets were in use and network operation was expected in the Midwest in 1949. *The New York Times'* prediction of three million sets in use by the end of 1949 was exceeded by half a million.[42] The use of AT&T's new Midwest coaxial cable was also a tremendous development in terms of network advertising. It provided an electrical connection from New York to such far-flung cities as Chicago, St. Louis and Milwaukee, and opened up these vast audiences to the network advertisers' message. The advertising agencies were excited. A major show such as the *Philco Television Playhouse* now went to 16 stations weekly and four additional ones on alternate weeks on kinescope film.[43]

The truest indications of television's fast and furious growth rate at this time were the reports on network advertising revenues. The sharp and dramatic changes justify regarding 1947–48 as the end of the period of early growth. From a gross business of $12 million in 1949, the networks jumped to gross billings of $127 million in 1952.[44] (In 1954 they were up to $320 million.) The big freeze and AT&T's cable proved a boon to those stations in operation, enabling them to increase audiences and revenues in a period of relative calm. By the 1950–51 season, at the tail-end of the freeze, every one of the 107 stations on the air claimed it was operating in the black.

Television drama began the era of the big freeze rather auspiciously. In the fall of the first season, 1948–49, costly dramatic shows were introduced on a permanent basis. The *Philco Television Playhouse* was first, with a budget that allowed it superior dramatic vehicles, and excellent talent. Then came *Ford Theater* and *Studio One*, both known for their quality and popular acceptance.[45] Altogether there were six major live dramatic shows on television as early as 1949.

These programs continued to present Broadway plays, but the increasing competition for hits suitable for television raised prices in what was a limited market.[46] *Philco* paid only $750 a script at first, but by the end of the season it was paying $2,000, with the cost of adaptation an extra expense.[47] New half-hour shows such as those sponsored by Chevrolet and Colgate reflected problems of limited running time and, together with the one hour shows, faced the problems of small budgets and little suitable material. Only a very limited number of one-act or full length plays worked on live television. The programmers were restricted by the need to use indoor settings as much as possible and only a limited number of these per play and by the censorship restrictions inherent in a mass media form of entertainment. The expanding half-hour series quickly gobbled up the meager supply of one-act plays and following the lead of ABC's Actors Studio, tapped a new source, the short story. *Kraft,* on the other hand, looked more and more to originals.

In spite of these problems the drama was a popular format with the programmers and, when grouped with dramatic films, shoved sports for the first time from first to third in the percentage of total broadcast time. Truly, television was doing for drama what radio had done for music. In contrast, musical programs on television started out strong but quickly deteriorated in number and quality. A more visual art, the opera, began to have a mild success on NBC, but CBS disbanded its symphony orchestra and made no attempts to produce opera.[48]

The critics, led by Jack Gould of *The New York Times,* hammered at those productions that merely photographed from a proscenium viewpoint. But he summarized the excitement over the "living" feature of broadcast drama:

> Its magic lies in the fact that it reaches mass audiences through mechanical means, yet it preserves the uninterrupted and instantaneous performance which is theater at its most credible. The uncertainty of a flubbed line can be the arresting attraction of television.[49]

With increased budgets came larger studios, more equipment, and a smoother, more polished and professional performance. NBC, of course, continued to dominate dramatic programming. CBS, however, is the more interesting topic for the first year of this middle period as it began its first full-scale assault on Rockefeller Center.

CBS and the Second "Civil War"

On May 4, 1944, one year before Japan surrendered, CBS reopened its Grand Central studios and assembled a new staff under the direction of Worthington Miner, a producer-director from Broadway. Thus it began its second "civil war" with NBC, a businesslike effort to do the best job and win the American public. CBS had successfully lured some major radio stars away from NBC but in the television area they had produced only a few half-hour dramas and mystery shows on a sustaining basis. However, in May of 1946, production ceased when Miner cancelled all live studio shows indefinitely in favor of old films and remote pick-ups of programs, usually athletic events from outside. They were cheaper and Miner was able to cut production costs in that early period. CBS simply did not have the resources of RCA. This changeover further delayed any extensive programming by CBS, and the first battle of the war was won by NBC.

Even though it was out of the picture as far as drama was concerned, in 1947 CBS made one highly publicized and fumbling attempt to telecast scenes from Broadway hits. It was called *Tonight on Broadway* and it featured *Mr. Roberts* in its premier broadcast. The reviewers described it as "amateurish television" that turned into a "fifty-minute advertising trailer for the play."[50] The American Tobacco Company dropped the sponsorship after three shows. CBS sustained three more before dropping the show—except for one brief attempt to revive it in the fall of 1949.[51]

In the first season of the big freeze, 1948–49, CBS was credited with a bid "to catch up" through its television version of the radio show, *Ford Theater*. This experiment by the Ford Motor Company, which had been a big spender on television for sports broadcasts, was a monthly venture alternating with a film theater and later in the season with *Studio One*.[52] With plays such as *The Man Who Came to Dinner* and *Edward, My Son*, and top stars, the show had a reasonably successful season and many viewers. Perhaps *Ford Theater*'s most unusual production was the result of an experiment in which the *Ford Radio Show* broadcast a version of *Camille* on November 12 with Ingrid Bergman, followed by a television version November 14 with Judith Evelyn. *Variety* agreed with the happy television producers who observed that "though the cards were stacked in advance for the radio program, with Ingrid Bergman playing the lead, the visual program won hands down over the aural."[53]

Because it passed from the scene after three seasons, the *Ford Theater* received little attention in subsequent years. Under the leadership of Garth Montgomery and director Marc Daniels, however, the Ford Motor Company cancelled the Ford radio theater and announced in the second season it would concentrate on *Ford Television Theater*, shifting to two programs a month and continuing with the same large budget.[54] *Variety* gave *Ford Theater* a Show Management Award for the 1949–50 season and described it as "one of the top video dramatic programs."⁵⁵ Marc Daniels, however, quit at the end of the season because he was refused the status of producer-director. Daniels went on to a successful career producing and directing other shows, but unlike the other brilliant young directors of television (Coe, Miner, Mc-Cleery), who moved up to producer status and gave their shows an identity and an individual purpose, Daniels was released and his original show died after him.⁵⁶ One interesting aspect of *Ford Television Theater*'s final season of "literal adaptations" was the hiring of Franklin Schaffner as the director. Schaffner had a successful career producing and directing on both networks after this apprenticeship with *Ford Theater;* he is most remembered for his *Hallmark Hall of Fame* shows.

If the *Ford Theater* fired the first shot, it was the honored and successful *Studio One* that fought the war. *Studio One* began its long career in 1948 with a title inherited from an old CBS radio show of Fletcher Markle's. This unit was the brain child of Worthington Miner, who had left the Theater Guild in 1939 to develop programs for CBS. Miner, a Phi Beta Kappa from Yale, came to television from the legitimate theater where he began his career in 1925 "carrying a spear" in a Walter Hampden road company. As a director, Miner staged more than 27 Broadway productions, including the Pulitzer Prize–winning *Both Your Houses.* Mr. Miner's assignment from CBS after World War II was to create four different types of shows. He was brilliantly successful in each and left a bright and indelible mark on the history of television.

The variety show he created was the *Toast of the Town,* in later days known as the *Ed Sullivan Show.* The situation comedy he created was *The Goldbergs;* the children's show he created was *Mr. I. Magination;* and finally, the one-hour quality drama he created was *Studio One.*⁵⁷

The premiere of *Studio One* on November 7, 1948, was *The Storm,* adapted by Worthington Miner from a novel by McKnight Malma. Margaret Sullivan and Dean Jagger starred and Miner directed. "Unfortunately," said *Variety,* "Studio One got off to a start that left the viewer both confused and bewildered."⁵⁸ This did not assuage Mr. Miner who stated vehemently that the reviewer's comment "needs clarification." In a conversation with this author, Miner explained:

> I was experimenting basically with adapting shows to a new medium. And in this first show I *deliberately* went out of my way to do a mystery story that would cause talk. This was deliberate. The show had no

ending; it left you in doubt. It was a *revolution* in techniques—in the mood lighting, in the use of the camera.[59]

For almost four years *Studio One* under the tutelage of Worthington Miner was hailed by critics and professionals alike for its slick professionalism and its daring production experiments. Television's first smash hit and Mr. Miner's most brilliant experiment was a modern dress version of Shakespeare's *Julius Caesar* in this very first season. The critics were generally overwhelmed! Gould portrayed it as "The most exciting television" he had seen:

> A magnificently bold, imaginative, and independent achievement....
> The visual power and vitality that lifted television to the status of a glorious art.[60]

Such words of praise as those had hardly been seen before. *Variety* agreed with him, pronouncing it a "big step forward. The fine integration of movement, lighting, camera, and staging . . . gave breadth and intensity to an exciting version of Shakespeare!"[61] This production was hailed across the country. The compliments were consistent: "One of television's memorable events"; "Extraordinary."[62]

Miner felt that this was the first application of the highly fluid storytelling technique of the television cameras to the classics. He was very delighted that Gould noticed and made mention of "An intelligent use of cameras to tell the story." For example, he told how they revealed to the audience their interpretation of Mark Anthony as a totalitarian:

> When Brutus was speaking to the crowd, in the rain with newspapers over their heads, we moved the camera through the crowd getting their reactions, and over behind the pillar was Mark Anthony, plotting his rebuttal. It was in his face—meditatively—we focused on him and we had it! He was played by Richard Hart. He was great![63]

Miner describes his use of the camera as an attempt to clarify. He felt that the best of camera work subsequently in television derives from this production. He describes one instance of using the cutting device to achieve a "theatrical wallop." The instance is the death of Cinna, the Poet. The camera cut from the fist of Cassius cursing and screaming at Brutus in the tent to the death scene: a man picks up a brick and slams it into Cinna's face; that is, right at the camera; the camera cuts and the dramatic statement has been made.

CBS sustained this expensive show until May of 1949 when Westinghouse picked up the sponsorship and kept it for nine and one half years until it went off the air in 1958. It was evidently a mutually beneficial relationship second only to the Kraft sponsorship of *Kraft Television Theater*. Several times throughout the following years it will be seen that Westinghouse and CBS changed producers, sometimes because they felt the quality of the show had fallen, but on the whole it seems to have been a very happy and distinguished relationship, with never a hint of bickering or sponsor interference.

The highlight of Studio One's second season was *The Battleship Bismarck*, one of television's first attempts at spectacular physical production. The Worthington Miner–Paul Nickell combination which had had such a great success with *Julius Caesar* in the first season of the big freeze, achieved, according to Gould, "a scope and variety of scene which suggested that television had barely begun to explore its own capabilities in the field of production."[64] The story concerned the fateful cruise of Germany's king-sized battleship, the *Bismarck*, and told of her successful engagements with the battleship *Hood* and the cruiser *Prince of Wales* and her eventual sinking by the British fleet. CBS newsman Larry LeSuer opened and closed the production so as to add authenticity.[65] Miner wrote about these pioneering activities:

> The fundamental fact . . . is that the Battleship Bismarck stood out for me as a symbol of escape from the strait-jacket of four-wall interiors, which had become an accepted limitation in television production up to that time. Many stories of fine quality, of valid interest had been turned down, solely because no workable production scheme had sprung to mind. More and more it appeared that the living room, the dining room, the office and the bar, were being frozen into the permanent habitat for every type of dramatic expression . . . [66]

Miner also felt that a show done later that season, *The Last Cruise*, was far more exciting technically, and went relatively unnoticed. He describes the *Battleship Bismarck* as "simple compared to *The Last Cruise*," in which a burning sub sank in the Arctic and a sister ship came to its rescue. "Eleven guys went to the doctor; we had one case of pneumonia and one broken leg. But we had two subs and we got them rocking in opposite directions!" One anecdote that Miner tells is that they never got the water until the very last rehearsal and they had never tested it on the floor. He said the water was within inches of shorting out the camera cables during the performance.

Worthington Miner's third season in *Studio One* saw his continued personal success. His productions continued to be mostly adaptations. Among these were *Jane Eyre*, Henry James' *The Ambassadors*, and a television version of Menotti's opera *The Medium*. He tells a story on himself about them. Miner felt that *Of Human Bondage* was his "biggest goof." He states:

> I had great success with adaptations of novels of Henry James—*The Ambassadors*, for example. These stories concerned a small number of people in a mass of extraneous material that can be caught by the television camera. So I got carried away and decided to do *Bondage*. This was a *fiasco*. I got a pretty good script from Sumner Locke Elliott, all things considered; but it had one fault—it was 27 minutes too long![67]

The year 1951–52 was Miner's final season with Studio One. He also felt it was one of his "best in terms of the quality of the shows. We had five knockout productions in a row." He particularly remembers *Waterfront Boss*, *Pontius Pilate*, and *Macbeth*. Miner was fascinated with *Waterfront Boss* because a lot of film was taken on the waterfront and he "couldn't get any police protection." He felt *Pontius Pilate* was one of the best scripts he had ever worked with, but "I made a mistake in casting Cyril Ritchard."[68]

Already in 1952 had come live television's third version of *Macbeth*, and there have been few like it before or since. Unlike Miner's previous Shakespearean productions, this was done in period costume. There were always reservations about Miner's "jazzing up the Bard."[69] It was one of the earliest television dramas seen by this writer and he remembers it as a provocative and exciting 60 minutes. It is easy when reviewing a production or writing in retrospect to remember it as a tour de force because of the production tricks, such as using prerecorded passages integrated with the live readings of the soliloquies and superimpositions of pictures to achieve the illusions of the ghostly dagger and the murdered Banquo, and it is easy to forget the impact and the intimacy that the television camera brought to the eternal *Macbeth*.

This was also Miner's final season with CBS. According to the newspapers he had been attempting to negotiate a new contract with CBS since July 1951, which would have given him the right to "expand into experimental and creative programming techniques." CBS reportedly stalled on his demands. According to *Variety* he met with NBC's Pat Weaver in January of 1952 and "set a deal on the spot." It was highly publicized throughout the industry that Worthington Miner would assume a major role in Weaver's "creative programming activities" at NBC.[70] Miner himself states that it was "simply a dispute over contract. . . . Mr. Weaver offered me more money." He was left to "cool his heels" for many years, however, and never did make a complete comeback. Some of Miner's later work on NBC will be discussed later in this book; also taken up will be Pat Weaver's explanation, "I bought the best" so the "others couldn't have them."

It was also a bad day for *Studio One.* Of the succeeding producers, Donald Davis was accused by reviewers of doing a particularly dull job and he was followed by Fletcher Markle who stayed for one year and went to Hollywood. It was not until Felix Jackson took over with Paul Nickell and Franklin Schaffner alternating as directors that the program regained the luster and pioneering nature that it had had under Worthington Miner. As Rod Serling described him in those years with *Studio One,* Miner was a "pioneer without coonskin, whose expanse was becoming as much horizontal as vertical."[71] As Miner put it, "we set the standards. It had a pattern. There was a bench mark of the kind of thing we wanted to do, and though we sometimes failed, we *never* compromised."[72]

Worthington Miner consistently attempted serious drama on a regular series basis, and very often succeeded, and seldom disregarded the mass entertainment features of the medium in which he was working. Those viewers and reviewers who contrasted Miner's success with the later success of Fred Coe on the *Philco Playhouse* like to point out that Fred Coe succeeded with more serious adult fare than any of those who were belittling the standards of television at that time could have imagined was possible, because he primarily sought to entertain. This is contrasted with Miner's use of esoteric and classical properties. In retrospect it hardly seems a fair comparison and perhaps is not even worth mentioning. The big difference was Miner's focus on adaptations and Coe's use of original materials. Another interesting difference between Coe's and Miner's approach to television drama is revealed by Miner himself and relates in a real way to the different production policies of NBC and CBS:

> NBC was under the control of RCA and they made a policy decision early in the game giving power to technical supervisors to countermand the Director's orders. CBS declared the Director supreme. No technical supervisor could ever countermand a director's orders; furthermore, directors had direct contact with the camera men. This gave us a whole

new dimension in adapting a show. We were able to explore "how to tell a story by camera." This contrasts with Fred Coe's putting his focus on developing a stable of writers. They were parallel developments. Coe would ask me about how we did this or that on a particular show — things which seem so simple today — pedestals in motion, raising and lowering cameras smoothly, low-key lighting. We were developing directors at CBS, men trained in the principles of directing, the use of cameras, mood lighting. For example, we had three outstanding directors refuse to direct the play of the week when we got in a jam and had to use the NBC studios.[73]

CBS's other two hour-long dramatic entries in the period of the big freeze were the *Magnavox Theater* and *Prudential Family Playhouse.* They had brief ordinary runs. The Prudential show, however, had quite a happy premiere with Gertrude Lawrence in S.N. Behrman's *Biography,* a performance that was typical of the vivacious and captivating Lawrence. Its quick death was occasioned by its placement opposite the popular NBC *Texaco Star Theater* with Milton Berle.[74]

Attempts by CBS to maintain the qualitative programming pace of NBC ran into considerable difficulties during these early years. Miner expressed the opinion that they were attributable to "lack of imagination at the executive level and a failure to develop and encourage talent." Certainly NBC had not only acquired a good head start on the other networks in the early years of programming on television, and it had continued to provide its personnel with the encouragement and the means to attempt the best. The big change at CBS would begin in 1950 when Hubbell Robinson, Jr., transferred to television from the position of vice president in charge of programming at CBS radio. This creative executive will be known as the man who created *Playhouse 90, Climax, 20th Century,* and the man who locked Phil Silvers and Nat Hicken in a hotel room until they created the great situation comedy starring Sgt. Bilko.

3
Entering the Fifties

The Half-Hour Series of 1949–50

One of the most noticeable features of dramatic programs from 1949–1951 was the emphasis on the half-hour live drama. This type of programming function passed quickly into the hands of the film-makers: a brief, slickly presented dramatic incident with room for a middle commercial. But in 1949 the producers were impressed with the successes of the live Colgate and Chevrolet shows, and the sponsors were impressed with their costs: $5,000 for the *Colgate Theater* and $6,000 for the *Chevrolet Tele-Theater*. Such low budgets made the half-hour drama easy to sell. *International Silver Theater, Big Story,* and *Lights Up* were offered in the fall of the 1949–50 season and in the summer the *Armstrong Circle Theater* and *Cameo Theater* got on the bandwagon. These half-hour series were a short-lived and unusual phenomenon.[1]

The *Chevrolet Tele-Theater,* or *Chevrolet on Broadway* as the program was originally titled, made its debut on the NBC network the previous season with the half-hour play *The Home Life of a Buffalo* by Richard Harrity. The story of a dancer and his family who refused to believe vaudeville was dead, it was a tried and proven script, having first been done on NBC television in 1946 and staged in a one-act playbill on Broadway in 1947. The play could hardly have missed for it used the same three leads from the earlier television and Broadway productions. The show and the series were instant successes. The show was produced by Owen Davis, Jr., and when he lost his life late in the season in a boating accident, he was succeeded by Victor McLeod.

33

McLeod's background in motion pictures enabled him to attract many Hollywood actors. Also many top stars were still appearing in many of these programs just to gain the experience in the new medium.[2] Chevrolet was followed in January of 1949 by an alternate Monday night half-hour drama, the *Colgate Theater,* also produced by McLeod and Davis.[3]

These were relatively inconspicuous series and this was a relatively inconspicuous format. They succeeded in a grand way for a few years because Hollywood's high-falutin' attitude and the high costs were delaying the use of film in television. The poor quality of reproduction may be conceded to be a factor in film's slow start, but more important is the fact that the cost per half-hour was well over $16,000 as compared to $6,000 or less for a half-hour live drama. So NBC decided to go "whole hog" and began in the late summer of 1949 with a series on NBC under the title *Lights Out,* produced by Fred Coe.[4] This series, *The Big Story,* and the *Armstrong Circle Theater* series differed from the conventional dramatic series in that they attempted a continuity of mood, theme, or style from production to production, much in the manner of the filmed situation comedies that became a major entertainment feature of television. They did not, however, fall into that class of comedy, mystery, or Western situation series that maintains the same hero from week to week in a new situation.

Coe had staged several *Lights Out* programs for NBC in 1947. This low budget program was based on the popular old radio series and was designed so that Coe could use experimental production techniques for the first time without fear of losing the audience or sponsor reprisals. The purpose of the show according to a publicity release was to do "psychological, mystery, and supernatural fare using adaptations and originals." The show was noted in successive seasons for its "first person" technique wherein the camera became the eyes of an unseen central character in the drama. It was also cited for the first utilization of a "split screen" technique; for example, when viewers witnessed simultaneously both sides of a telephone conversation of a frantic wife who is trying to save her husband from the electric chair.[5]

An original script written by Fred Coe in December 1947 was very unusual in consideration of Coe's subsequent career as the leading light of original television drama. One must in good humor guess that this led him to decide to become a writer's producer rather than a writer's director. It is the story of a television director who gets his just desserts for cutting and rewriting an original play beyond recognition. The characters, "almost frighteningly alive" in the first draft, actually do materialize and attempt to intimidate the director into going back to the original. "You've cut us out from our story!" they cry. The director insists the play go on as it is, but he pays with his life when the characters murder him![6] Evidently Coe decided in 1950 to "save his life" and not overdo rewriting originals. From this point onward Coe would be known in the industry as a writer's producer and would make a special contribution to television through his work with his "stable" of young television writers.

Several other NBC half-hour series had a decent success. *The Big Story* was based on the radio production of the same name and its stories were derived from accounts of newspapermen who had performed public service. It popularized the use of film clips. Two that were eventually published were *The Julian Housman Story* and *The Kathryn Steffan Story,* the titles bearing the names of the reporter being recognized.

The *Armstrong Circle Theater,* with Hudson Faussett as the producer, offered sentimentality with "the pleasantly related moral" as the show's thematic approach. This "family type drama" concentrated on sentimental fiction and real life stories and eventually resulted in a one hour series that lasted until 1954. A typical example might be *The Rocking Horse,* which told of a mother and her son's tender reunion after 25 years because of a rocking horse the son recognized.

In many ways the *Lights Out* series should be regarded as the most successful of the half-hour programs premiered by NBC during the big freeze, mostly because of its production experiments, but in its second season it ranked eighth in a national popularity poll, and it acquired a sponsor, the Admiral Corporation.[7] NBC dropped its half-hour Colgate and Chevrolet series in their second season, but the half-hour format received fresh interest from the many new arrivals on CBS the following season: *Lux Video Theater, The Web, Danger,* and the *Somerset Maugham Theater.* Competition between the giants of broadcasting was, as always, a significant influence in terms of progress. CBS again showed its determination to better the dramatic programming activities of NBC through the half-hour shows above and the two previously mentioned hour-long series: *The Magnavox Theater* and the *Prudential Family Playhouse.*

Actually CBS's half-hour series did not fare well with the reviewers.

Lux Video Theater was intended as a television version of *Lux Radio Theater,* which had had a phenomenal 15-year success in radio, often being on top of the Hooper and Nielsen ratings.[8] The J. Walter Thompson Agency was having similar success with *Kraft Television Theater* and decided to move *Lux* to television as it had done on radio. The premiere of the new series was Maxwell Anderson's *Saturday's Children,* which was edited down to a half-hour. John Crosby, the television reviewer for the *New York Herald Tribune,* was often "cute" in his reviews and he seems less quotable than Jack Gould of the *Times* in terms of what actually happened. But Gould did occasionally make fun of television and in this review he was concerned with "obscure" motivations and characterizations "evidently mislaid at the story conference," but his prize comment concerned the commercial:

> Joan Caufield merits considerable applause for her reading of a difficult commercial. Even though this is the year 1950, she had to say the following: "Wherever I am and whatever part I play, I'll be a Lux girl. It's a wonderful soap."[9]

CBS' second new half-hour series, the *Somerset Maugham Theater,* was quite successful until it ran out of material as a natural consequence of its relatively short format. To utilize Maugham's novels, this series was expanded in April of that season to an hourly version. The revised series opened with a performance of *Of Human Bondage.* R.L. Shayon of the *Saturday Review* tended to be harsh and pedantic in his occasional television reviewing but he was particularly vitriolic about *Of Human Bondage:*

> the wickedest sin . . . was not the audacious attempt . . . it was not the outrageous commercial . . . the basic transgression . . . was the rape of the spirit and meaning of Maugham's novel. . ., the hero's search . . . was scaled down to an insipid version. . .[10]

This was quite strong stuff and if the writer may be allowed a "basic transgression," it was not unusual. Shayon did once in a fit of good humor describe a *Robert Montgomery Presents* production of F. Scott Fitzgerald's *The Last Tycoon* as a "first rate performance." He also described this television adaptation as one that "respected the author's approach and communicated it to video with taste and imagination."[11]

Shayon's comments were actually a come-on for he had not discontinued his sullen ways. The above comment was contained in a column in which he expressed intense dislike of six hourly television dramas of the previous two weeks. On an earlier occasion Shayon expressed a preference for radio drama and expressed a "dim view" of stage plays on television in a still earlier column because of an "inevitable thinning out process."[12] Many of Shayon's comments seem exaggerated, but it is certain that the programmers were relying on adaptations of novels and biographies and the "thinning out" process warranted some of his negative reactions. Robert Lewine, an NBC vice president, accurately described these years as television drama's "dull" period, "the gathering of energy and experience and the calm of adapting others' works before the storm of original creations."[13]

ABC Enters the Race

ABC made a late start in dramatic programming in the 1950–51 season and it never got to the finish line. The venture, which was quite a memorable one, was *Schlitz Pulitzer Prize Playhouse*.[14] Actually, the American Broadcasting Company had made a half-hearted attempt at dramatic programming in the first season of the big freeze, 1948–49, with a half-hour series, *Actor's Studio*, which ran for two years. In the tradition of the now famous Actors Studio of New York, ABC presented realistic plays successfully under the joint sponsorship of the Actors Studio, World Video Company, and ABC. Since Actor's Studio was more of an informal gathering of theater artists for the mutual self-improvement than a formal producing organization, it did not produce these plays in the usual sense of the word, as, for example, the Theater Guild produced the *U.S. Steel Hour*. Rather, actors associated with the Studio lent their time and talents to the series' productions at low salaries to achieve experience in the television medium.[15] This series received national recognition as the first television program ever to be honored by the distinguished Peabody Award, cited for "uninhibited and brilliant pioneering in telecast drama," as "the first to recognize that drama on television is neither a stage play nor a movie, but a separate and distinct new art form."[16] Donald Davis, *Actor's Studio* producer, spoke about their pioneering activities:

> When Actor's Studio first went on the air, there were, up to then,
> very few if any, dramatic shows which ever attempted to do more than

put cut versions of old plays in front of the TV cameras. . . . We hit on
what was then considered a novel idea . . . the short story.[17]

Actor's Studio was a low budget sustaining show in the sense of
the early experiments on NBC. The Schlitz Brewery Company's venture
with *Pulitzer Prize Playhouse* was quite different. This ambitious project was under the management of the William Morris Agency and had
the cooperation of the Columbia University Graduate School of Journalism, which had received a $100,000 gift from the Schlitz Company.
The opening production was Kaufman and Hart's *You Can't Take It
with You*. Despite the series' successes, it lost its sponsor at the end of
the season because of "a lack of available dramatic properties."[18]

The show's format posed limitations and problems similar to those
that beset the *Somerset Maugham Theater*. During the year it was
forced to present many dramas which were not Pulitzer Award winners,
but by authors who had been cited by the Pulitzer Committee. ABC
was still the "baby network" of the television industry and did not yet
have the audience potential to keep a big advertiser tied to a high
budgeted show. Schlitz planned instead for the 1951–52 season to move
to CBS with its larger network and to produce a new dramatic series
called *Schlitz Playhouse of Stars* which would replace the *Ford Theater*
on Fridays. No less a group of authorities than Fred Coe, Worthington
Miner, and David Suskind[19] have been quoted to the effect that ABC
was very much responsible for the death of live drama in 1958 because
of its low-grade competition in the form of Western dramas. It should
be noted, however, that in 1950–51 and successive seasons, ABC made
attempts to produce and compete on the same level as the two big networks with brilliant and quality productions in series such as the
Pulitzer Prize Playhouse, Celanese Theater, and the *Steel Hour*. In all
three instances ABC demonstrated creativity at the executive level;
shows did not last, however, or as in the case of the *Playhouse* and the
Steel Hour, moved to one of the big networks.

The Big Thaw

The thawing out of the FCC freeze was the beginning of the end
of Broadway revivals on live television. The three short years of this big
freeze saw television become a colossus of the world of entertainment

and saw live television drama increasingly dominate programming activities. The most durable form of television program was the straight drama and it was consistently the highest rated program category in the A.C. Nielsen audience surveys.[20]

The problems television drama had in this period were the usual desperate search for story material and the continued cry of the critics against ruthlessly skimpy and unfair condensations of full length works. Television was quickly using up the available material and many works that were potentially good drama were not usable because their authors were afraid of television, or copyright laws made presentation prohibitively expensive or impossible. As it exhausted the supply of obvious revivals of three-act plays, television experimented with one-act plays, short stories, novels, biographies, and royalty-free literary classics. Shakespeare, Molière, and the nineteenth century novelists were fair game, and NBC's summer show, *Masterpiece Playhouse,* did television productions of dramatic classics by Ibsen, Chekhov, and Pirandello.

This *Masterpiece Playhouse* replaced the *Philco* show and was one of a number of summer hiatus shows that were usually experimental and usually sustaining. One such show was Worthington Miner's *CBS Workshop* where top young directors were to receive valuable training. The *Masterpiece Playhouse* is particularly noteworthy because the producers were Yale University's Curtis Canfield, Fred Coe, and Albert McCleery, and they adapted such famous plays as *Hedda Gabler, The Rivals, Richard III, Six Characters in Search of an Author, Othello,* and *Uncle Vanya.* The series received mixed reviews and even this viewer was somewhat disappointed and seemed less inclined than ever before to excuse production errors on the basis of experimentation in a new medium. *Six Characters in Search of an Author* was particularly bad but the off-stage antics would have delighted Pirandello! If the reader does not already know it, the play presents several levels of reality and poses the question "What is real?" Instead of a bare stage it was presented in a bare video studio. Therefore rather than use a stage doorman to interrupt the action, the director decided to use an NBC page. When the question of casting the page came up someone suggested that there was a boy on the page staff that wanted to be an actor by the name of Ericksen and he received the part. After the show was over the wardrobe mistress asked the page to turn in his costume. He replied, "No, it's mine; I own it." She *insisted* and he *insisted* right back that he had to go to work in it the next day. Being very determined, she called over a script girl and requested that she support her argument, to which the script girl replied that she didn't know anything about it—she wasn't a script girl—she was an actress playing a script girl![21]

On the whole, however, the best television drama was still a rehash of Broadway successes. On the creative side, very little had happened since the initial experiments in camera techniques. Most television drama in this middle period was a mere cataloguing of Broadway adaptations. The saturation point of adaptations had been reached, and drama was more popular than ever. It suddenly became painfully evident that television drama would have to shut up shop unless more material was unearthed. A producer, Stanley Quinn of the *Kraft* show, explained: "The originals we get usually were turned down by the theater or the movies."[22] Another producer, Robert Montgomery, blamed the writers: "We don't have enough original plays submitted to us for consideration." His program used only six originals in the 1951–52 season, and they were his first such attempts.[23] Producer Fred Coe in 1954 gave the best summary of television drama's problems at this point and their eventual solution:

> When the "Playhouse" did its first show in October 1948, all of us were convinced it was our mission to bring Broadway to America via the television set. And so we drew our material from the Broadway Theater. We took Broadway plays, trimmed them to an hour and cast them with Broadway players, topped by a Broadway star. Within a couple of months it became obvious that this could not work out. We were running out of material! Broadway did 50 or 60 plays a year, many of which were unsuitable or unavailable for our show...
>
> Meanwhile other dramas were emerging on television. The shortage of material became acute. Agents stalked archives, bought rights to stories and novels in umpteen languages, toured obscure libraries here and abroad searching, searching for words to fill the void.
>
> And soon, logically, we had worked out our present "Television Play" setup in which we use virtually nothing but originals. Our writers turn out *television plays* in every sense of the phrase.... Our emphasis is now almost completely on the original television play, and in the process we have developed a group of television playwrights.[24]

Within a few years new plays and new writers such as Reginald Rose, Rod Serling, Paddy Chayefsky, Tad Mosel, Horton Foote, and Robert Alan Aurthur would answer the television dramatic series' most pressing need and bring to them original creation in a "new art."

4
The 1951–52 and
1952–53 Seasons

High Noon in New York

The television networks launched their seventh year of postwar commercial telecasting with the first live transcontinental television program on September 4, 1951, President Truman's address at the Japanese peace conference. This opening-up of the West Coast eventually had a marked effect on television. Already there were signs that the top variety shows would come from Hollywood and dramatic shows would begin to appear on the Coast which used the stars from the motion picture industry. Live television, however, and live original television drama from New York were to be the significant money-making features of prime time network television for at least five more years. During that time the network's income continued its fantastic rise while the motion picture industry watched its income drop faster every day. Network radio was dead for most purposes. Jack Benny's radio show, for example, had a rating of 26.5 in 1948. Its rating in 1951 was 4.8.[1] *Variety* labeled television the "monster" and wondered "will TV eventually swallow up practically all of show business?" The "worst" was yet to come!

On April 14, 1952, the FCC ended its three and a half year ban on new television stations with its "Sixth Report and Order" allowing for 2,053 new stations blanketing the country and reserving 242 for educational use.[2] The freeze had been originally imposed to eliminate station interference and to set a pattern for future expansion. The resolution arranged for maximum use of the band of frequencies then in use, VHF or very high frequencies, and opened a new band of frequencies, UHF or ultra high frequencies. In the next six months, 175 new television stations were authorized and within a year the number of stations broadcasting had doubled. By 1954, over 393 stations were on the air, and television set ownership rose to 35 million.[3] By 1955, television became a billion dollar industry and the networks were able to undertake programming on a larger scale than anyone previously had imagined.[4] Within a single decade television had established itself as the dominent mass communications medium of our time.

As television grew it became, along with public education, one of America's favorite critical targets. As the major mass medium it received much blame for the social and cultural evils of a mass society. The television industry, through the National Association of Radio and Television Broadcasters, tried to protect itself from public criticism by adopting a Television Code in 1951. Robert Swezy, chairman of the NARBT at that time, admitted:

> To a great extent, however, it (the television code) was adopted under the threat of government censorship of the medium; i.e. the Benton Bill which provided for the establishment of a citizen's committee to review and make recommendations to the Congress concerning television programming.[5]

This Code urged adherence to "decency and decorum in production" and was generally negative in approach. It had very little effect on programming through the years. Such concern for the social effects of this mushrooming monster resulted in a Ford Foundation study and eventually the famous Omnibus Show.[6]

Dawn in Hollywood

If live television had its "high noon" in New York in the early fifties, there was a bit of "dawn" in Hollywood. Abel Green and Joe Laurie, Jr., in their book *Show Biz from Vaude to Video,* described the 1951–52 season as the "year of decision" for the moviemakers. Major film studios were beginning to rent space for television film production. Also many film moguls were investigating the possibilities of producing such films themselves.[7] When the freeze had ended and television had doubled and tripled in size, the moviemakers finally realized that they must join forces with this "monster" in order to survive. The results of this reversal in policy were seen as early as July 1952 when *Variety* reported that television films on the networks had grown in the previous season from 12 hours weekly to 18, a 50 percent increase, and added a separate review section called Telepix Reviews.[8]

What was even more shocking to the dévotés of live drama was that for the first time since television had started there were no new live dramatic series announced that September.[9] The trade newspapers boldly announced that the celluloid era in television had arrived. Also the reviewers were worried that the quality of the returning live drama had fallen. Each major dramatic program could point to individual productions of which it had reason to be proud, but none had maintained the consistent excellence of *Celanese Theater* of 1951–52 or the pioneering *Philco* or *Studio One* shows in their early years. Jack Gould of the *Times* practically panicked:

> The medium is heading hell-bent for the rut of innocuity, mediocrity, and sameness that made a drab if blatant jukebox of radio. Morning, noon, and night the channels are cluttered with eye-wearying monstrosities called 'films for TV,' half-hour aberrations that in story and acting would make an erstwhile Hollywood producer of 'B' pictures shake his head in dismay.[10]

Such anxiety was perhaps well founded, for as one television producer, D.W. Sharpe, commented when asked by Gould about the terrible quality of the films Hollywood was grinding out: "I'm so busy [making them], I just don't have time to watch them."[11] By 1965, the filmed situation comedy would dominate television programming with 40 plus series that season. For the present these two sample seasonal lineups reveal the hard times they were having:

1950	*1952*
Beulah	Abbott & Costello
Easy Aces	Boss Lady
George Burns & Gracie Allen	Date with Judy
The Girls	Dave and Charley
Pinky Lee Show	Life with Luigi
Hank McCune Show	Leave It to Larry
Stu Erwin Show	It's a Business
Peter Lind Hayes Show	Those Endearing Young Charms
Menasha the Magnificent	My Little Margie
	Mr. Peepers

(cont.)	1950	1952
		Papa Cellini
		My Friend Irma
		Heaven for Betsy
		Adventures of Ozzie & Harriet
		Our Miss Brooks
		Doc Corkle
		I Married Joan
		Meet Millie
		My Hero

The titles tell the story. Most of them were superficial, simplistic pap with stereotyped characters and pallid plots. In a few years *Variety* would report bankruptcies, mergers, and general turbulence among the independent ("B") moviemakers that had been trying "to make a fast buck."[12]

Thus the shouting about film was premature. Aside from the relatively high budgets and low picture quality of most of the filmed dramatic series, there was a dynamic creative force ready to explode in the television industry. This creative force was furthered and nourished chiefly by the same pioneering series and advertising agencies that had popularized the live, hour drama — the *Philco Television Playhouse* and the J. Walter Thompson Agency through its *Lux Video* and *Kraft Television* theaters. On these shows there appeared by 1953 original television plays by authors such as Horton Foote, Paddy Chayefsky, Tad Mosel, Rod Serling, and Robert Alan Aurthur. Others would appear in the next few years, including Reginald Rose and J.P. Miller. These and the many other fine writers of original television drama were youths who had developed their talents working in the television industry, many of them by writing the adaptations of the preceding seasons. Now the television industry needed them.

It was not film but live television drama that continued to dominate prime time programming in the next period.

The Measure of Excellence

The Broadway theater was still the measure of excellence in 1951, not movies. Nor had television drama achieved an identity of its own. It was that way, then, when ABC made a brilliant effort to compete with NBC and CBS. In the field of hour-long television drama, where the competition was unusually keen, the *Celanese Theater* of ABC achieved exciting success and for one brief year established a preeminence in quality programming. It was a package show from the William Morris talent agency which had access to the long, venerable list of Broadway hits by the playwrights identified with the Playwrights Company—Maxwell Anderson, Philip Barry, Elmer Rice, Robert E. Sherwood, S.N. Behrman, and Eugene O'Neill. In fact, it was originally to be called the Celanese Playwright's Theater.[13]

Much of the credit for the *Celanese* success went to Jerry Stagg, head of program development for the William Morris Agency, who signed up the properties of a number of distinguished playwrights. He put himself in such an enviable position, in the vital area of program materials, by drawing up a season's schedule a year ahead. Credit also goes to Alex Segal, the producer-director, and future *Hallmark Hall of Famer,* who had handled 1950–51's *Pulitzer Prize Playhouse* on ABC.[14] With the scripts of proven successes in hand, the battle was half won. Jack Gould in the *Times* portrayed Alex Segal as "one of the most deft and discerning directors in television's ranks, . . . bringing these hits to the screen with remarkable faithfulness."[15] For the second time the George Foster Peabody Award honored a television dramatic series and again it was an ABC show.[16] At that period of great critical concern over television's poorly executed adaptations, it is interesting that this Peabody award credited the *Celanese Theater* with drama "done with fidelity, intelligence, and scrupulous regard for the intentions of the playwright." The high culture elitists and television professionals who criticized ABC in later years did not give it enough credit. The "big boys" would not let the "little guy" play the game. We shall see how ABC eventually lands the Disney film show, introduces the film Western and chases the "big boys" right out of the ball park.

Celanese Theater also received a special citation in *Variety's* Showmanagement Awards:

> In a season which saw television's hour long dramatic shows come into their own as the best in qualitative programming, ABC-TV's "Celanese Theater" quickly established itself as tops. . .
>
> Alex Segal directed . . . with imagination, plus production and direction know-how. . . . He embellished for "Celanese" the comparatively new concept of camera technique—that of shooting from all four sides of a set. The smooth and easy flow of his camera movements often compensated for static qualities in a script.[17]

DuMont Who . . . ?

Also in the early fifties the small DuMont television network made a feeble attempt to get into "big league" television drama with the high budgeted *Cosmopolitan Theater,* packaged by the Louis G. Cowan Agency for DuMont on a sustaining basis. These were the most lavish productions ever attempted by DuMont, with scripts based on stories from *Cosmopolitan* magazine.[18] A sponsor was not found and the show closed by December.[19]

A more interesting attempt at television drama was made by Du-Mont that season on a local basis in New York City. The series was called *Broadway Theater* and the producer was Warren Wade, who had been one of NBC's first production chiefs. Under Wade's direction each play was performed five nights a week in a full length, 90-minute to two-hour version. This format attracted considerable attention because of a feeling that so many programs "go down the drain" as far as the individual set owner was concerned. A survey made for DuMont by Pulse, Inc., revealed the five performances of the opening production, *The Trial of Mary Dugan,* reached a larger percentage of television homes than any other show that week including those on the networks.[20] Wade continued to produce these shows for two seasons on a local basis. From the very beginning he faced the problem of acquiring rights to suitable plays, and he never did achieve financing on a network basis.[21]

The Golden Age of Live Television

Live, original television charged onto the screen in the early fifties and live television drama finally achieved an identity of its own. The years 1951 through 1956 were a time wherein television made a significant contribution to the arts in the form of the original television play. Rod Serling, one of television's most successful writers, described television's entry into the playwriting business in 1951:

> The medium had progressed somewhat past the primitive stage. . . .
> The television writer's claim to the title "playwright" had been made
> but as yet was not universally accepted. The television play . . . enjoyed
> no longevity through the good offices of the legitimate stage and the
> motion picture. The motion picture industry looked down on its

newborn cousin somewhat as the president of a gourmet club might examine an aborigine gnawing a slab of raw meat.[22]

In describing the "black desert which represented the area of identity of the television writer" in 1951, Serling used the *Kraft Television Theater* as an illustration, stating this oldest of the one-hour shows was better than most producing units in its treatment of writers but even it would not permit a writer at rehearsal until the day of the performance.[23] The great change that came about in the treatment of the writer can be discovered by examining Serling's impromptu recollections of these years, and he stated the results clearly:

> The major advance in the television play was a thematic one. . . . One could see that the television play was beginning to show depth and a preoccupation with character. Its plots and its people were becoming meaningful. Its stories had something to say. . .
>
> In terms of technique, the "close-up" that had served as such a boon to the motion pictures was further refined and used to even greater advantage in television. The key to television drama was intimacy. . .[24]

Serling was describing the realistic, intimate drama found on television from the period 1952 to 1956 that came to be called "adult" drama. Ring Lardner offered a reason as to why it came about:

> In a mass medium where writer's work is consumed at a ravenous rate, the lure of the socially significant becomes more than the veriest hack can resist. The cute premises about amnesia and double identities grow strained after a while.[25]

Whatever the reasons for the forms original television dramas began to take, it was certain in 1951–52 why they began to be produced. The alternative to their use by the dramatic series was to close up shop. While Robert Montgomery had blamed the writers in 1950–51 for not submitting scripts, their reasons for not doing so seem valid: market prices for a one-hour original went up from $750 in 1950–51 to $2,000 in 1951–52.[26] Before 1950 it simply had not been worth the aspiring writer's time because the pay was too low.

The change from adaptations to original drama was so sudden that the summer of 1952 was a storehouse of original television plays in contrast to the drab adaptations of the previous fall. The summer season was normally a time when most shows either went off the air, lowered their budgets, or played reruns; but that summer, under the new impetus to produce originals, the following plays were produced: *Expec-*

tant Relations, Tears of My Sister, and *The Death of the Old Man* by
Horton Foote; *The Rack* and *Old MacDonald Had a Curve* by Rod Serl-
ing; *Ernie Barger Is Fifty* and *Other People's Houses* by Tad Mosel; and
The Big Deal by Paddy Chayefsky.

Fred Coe and the Playwrights

Theater-trained Fred Coe was hired by WNBT back in April of
1945 and directed his first play for television for a late afternoon
children's show, a television version by Ben Martin of DeMaupassant's
The Necklace. With Fred Coe as the producer-director, NBC would
take the leading role in projecting television into a big-time operation
and the leading role in making drama its number one format. During
these "glory" years he will be personally identified with many of live
television's greatest triumphs.

On September 17, 1952, the *Philco Playhouse* produced the first
play of the first playwright to achieve fame through the television
medium. The playwright was Paddy Chayefsky, an aspirant to legitimate playwriting, and the play was *Holiday Song.* It was produced by
Fred Coe and directed by Gordon Duff. It was repeated September 20,
1953, with script revisions and casting changes in commemoration of
the Jewish High Holy Days.[27]

By the end of that season Chayefsky was joined in Coe's *Philco
Playhouse* "stable" by Horton Foote, Robert Alan Aurthur, Thomas
Phipps, and Tad Mosel. This first play, *Holiday Song,* was "ostensibly
an adaptation" of an article in the *Reader's Digest,* but Chayefsky felt
that after revisions and changes he had written "what amounts to a
completely original work." It is the story of a gentle, middle-aged cantor who becomes distraught and disillusioned over the misery and sad-
ness in the world, especially the antisemitism. Believing that he has
"lost his faith," he feels he cannot rightfully perform his duties during
the Rosh Hashanah services, and consequently takes his problem to a
leading rabbi in nearby Manhattan. But enroute he is twice directed by
a mysterious subway guard into the wrong Brooklyn train. The first
time he meets a woman refugee, and the second time her long lost husband. As a result, he reunites them and renews his faith.[28] *Variety*
misspelled the name of this new writer as Paddy Chayepsky, but felt
he had written "one of its [Philco's] more moving vehicles."[29]

Chayefsky's second television play, *Printer's Measure*, was produced on the *Playhouse* in April. It is the story of how a linotype
machine affects the life of an elderly printer by shattering, not only his
confidence in his craft, but also his relationship with his apprentice,
who gradually transfers his hero worship to the new machine. Chayefsky felt: "It has neither the honesty of *Marty* nor half the characterizations that went into *The Bachelor Party* and *The Mother,* but it has
solid architecture and I like it."[30] It is basically a character study, showing a crisis in the emotional relationship of the man and the boy, but
it also has a social significance, for the old printer stands for the dying
artisan in the world of machines.

This play was followed in May by the now famous *Marty,* with its
echoing lines: "Well, what do you feel like doing tonight?" and its con-
trary answer, "I don't know. What do you feel like doing?" Marty, a
butcher in his middle thirties, has none of the social graces and is
tormented by the emptiness and loneliness portrayed in the dialogue
with his bachelor friend. In a cheap dance hall he finds a gangling,
awkward girl, and the substance of Chayefsky's story is their discovery
that they have a rapport and when they are together, there is a meaning
in life.[31] Much has been written about *Marty* since it won the Academy
Award as a movie. Ernest Borgnine won fame and fortune in the leading role. At its first performance on television Gould commented
favorably on its "touching pathos" and Chayefsky's "disciplined appreciation of reality in every day life."[32] *Marty* was the grand debut of
a new style of drama. In his book Chayefsky bundled together *Marty*
and *The Mother*[33] in one discussion of this style because he said "each
represents in its own way the sort of material that does best on television":

> They [*Marty* and *The Mother*] both deal with the world of the mun-
> dane, the ordinary, and the untheatrical. The main characters are
> typical, rather than exceptional; the situations are easily identifiable by
> the audience; and the relationships are as common as people. The
> essence of these two shows lies in their literal reality. I tried to write the
> dialogue as if it had been wire-tapped. I tried to envision the scenes as
> if a camera had been focused upon the unsuspecting characters and had
> caught them in an untouched moment of life.
> This sort of meticulous literalness is something that can be done in
> no other medium. On the stage, reality is a highly synthesized thing.
> The closest thing to reality I ever saw on the stage was in *Death of a
> Salesman,* but even this extraordinary play involved a suicide and an

incident in which the son discovers his father in a hotel room with a
woman other than his mother. These are excellent dramatic incidents,
but they are not everyday occurrences in the life of the lowermiddle
class. In writing the stage play, it is necessary to contrive exciting
moments of theater. You may write about ordinary people, but the audience sees them in unordinary and untypical circumstances.

To a lesser degree, this is also true of the movies, especially American
movies. *The Bicycle Thief*, an Italian masterpiece, got about as close to
an ordinary day in unemployed man's life as you can get in a movie;
but even this picture required a special urgency of incident. Most
movies, even the good ones, are based upon the extraordinary incident
and the exceptional character.

In television, however, the same insights into a character or into a
social milieu can be made with the most identifiable characters and the
most commonplace situations. I set out in *Marty* to write a love story,
the most ordinary love story in the world. I didn't want my hero to be
handsome, and I didn't want the girl to be pretty. I wanted to write a
love story the way it would literally have happened to the kind of people
I know. I was, in fact, determined to shatter the shallow and destructive
illusions—prospered by cheap fiction and bad movies—that love is
simply a matter of physical attraction, that virility is manifested by a
throbbing phallus, and that regular orgasms are all that's needed to
make a woman happy.[34]

Marty was followed shortly in July by *The Big Deal*, with David
Opatoshu playing "the big deal," a man of 52, a one-time "big shot,"
as he calls himself, who yearns for the day when he was a big builder
of homes. Now he must rely on the financial support of his daughter
while he dreams up pretentious and impractical projects. He is seen
gradually becoming aware he is a failure and finally accepting a low
paid job.[35] Opatoshu's performance and Vincent Donahue's direction
were hailed by the critics as "painfully real." *Variety* said: "Not once
was there a false note. . . . With so brilliant a cast and Chayefsky's un-
commonly perceptive script to work with, Director Vincent Donahue
achieved strong impact and perfect pacing."[36] With this production
Chayefsky finished his first season as a playwright to almost universal
acclaim: Gould spoke of his "disciplined appreciation of reality"; John
Crosby in the *New York Herald Tribune* described him as "television's
best writer"; and *Variety* commented: "Chayefsky . . . makes a habit
of writing for TV as if he invented the medium."[37]

Horton Foote was the second writer to achieve fame on the Philco
show that season. His two most important productions were *The Trip
to Bountiful* which was written for Lillian Gish and was later the first

television play produced on Broadway,[38] and *A Young Lady of Property*, a vignette about a teenage girl's dreams, loneliness, and growing pains in a small town in 1925.[39] The success of these two plays formed the basis for a series of dramas by Foote on small town life in *Harrison, Texas*, the title of the published series. The plays were of the same style as Brooklynite Chayefsky's dramas about lower middle class city life, except that Foote's intimacy and vividness reflected a different, rural breed of folk.

Several of these dramas by Foote were featured on another NBC experimental summer series called *First Person*, directed by the man, himself, Fred Coe. In it, a central character was represented by both the eye of the camera and an actor. When the actor was heard but not seen, the other characters looked and talked directly to the camera. This notion was not a new one, but *Variety* credited Coe and his other director, Arthur Penn, with using it "in a fresh way that opens fresh horizons to television drama."[40] Foote's *Tears of My Sister*, for example, told in a tender way the story of a young girl forced to marry a much older and unwanted man, so that she could provide for her mother and sister. It was told through the viewpoint of the younger sister, represented by the camera with Kim Stanley's voice.[41]

The third exciting young playwright to be discovered by *Philco Playhouse* that season was a find of the show's summer producer. The playwright was Tad Mosel, and his first hour-long original to be produced on television was done on assignment for David Suskind, who was producing *Television Playhouse* during Fred Coe's summer absence. The play was *Ernie Barger Is Fifty*, and on the basis of its success Mosel was brought into Coe's "stable" and given a playhouse contract.

Ed Begley played Ernie Barger in the personal tragedy of an amiable, hard-working man who discovers at the age of fifty that he is no longer needed in his pottery factory, and that his son has grown up and is breaking away from him. He has been ignoring his wife and father and pinning his hopes on his son. When in despair he turns to them, he discovers that his father has found a lonely life for himself and does not need his love, and his wife has turned away from him and into a hypochondriac, because he failed to give her attention.[42] This writer attests to a very moving production and the reviewers agreed. Ed Begley was great. The play's style and quality were close to Chayefsky's and Foote's. For all three of these writers the keynote was sensitivity on the part of the writer's techniques, character studies in terms of play materials, pathos in terms of purpose, and intimate realism in terms of style.[43] In discussing his plotting and characterizations Mosel wrote much in the same vein as Chayefsky:

> Never before has there been a medium so suited to what I call the "personal drama" — that is, a play wherein the writer explores one simple happening, a day, or even an hour, and tries to suggest a complete life. . . . The life may be an unimportant one, but it implies a community, which in turn implies the world.[44]

He makes a further correlation in terms of his audience:

> If I consciously tried to write for an audience of that size [average at this time was about twenty million] I wouldn't know where to begin. I much prefer to believe the exact opposite, which in this age of paradoxes, is also true — that television is the most intimate entertainment medium ever conceived: three or four people in a living room, settled low in their favorite chairs, watching a 21-inch screen.[45]

Edmund Rice of *Kraft Television Theater* fame was the first to describe a television performance in this manner. He was so quoted in *Best Television Plays* published in 1950 and restated when interviewed that he felt the essential difference between motion picture and television writing is that for the first time a play is seen by three or four people only. When asked about this description he commented:

> I still feel strongly that this is true. You have an enormous audience in *toto*, but you are playing to a small audience actually. The small reactions, feelings, and emotions are thus more important than the broad action, the big, broad scope.[46]

Although they received little public recognition, Fred Coe had another "stable" of artists, his *Philco Playhouse* directors, Delbert Mann, Vincent Donahue, Arthur Penn and Gordon Duff. All three playwrights who debuted that 1952–53 season took great pains when discussing their reactions to rehearsals and live performances to give most of the credit to these directors' ability to interpret and realize the best that was in their dramas, and, of course, Fred Coe gave them full responsibility for his success. All of them went on to successful careers in the theater, television, and the movies.

In discussing *The Lawn Party*, a play of the 1953–54 season, Mosel gives some idea of the work of two of these men:

Arthur Penn directed *The Lawn Party.* I can't begin to say how much I rely on a director. I like to give him my play unconditionally to do with as he sees fit. This can be dangerous if he doesn't speak my language. So far I have worked with Delbert Mann four times and with Arthur Penn five. I can only say that I would willingly entrust any play to either one of them at any time. Arthur always announces at the first rehearsal that he is not quite sure what the play is about. This sometimes startles the actors, but it pleases me. Because there is an anticipation in his voice, an eagerness to get to work, and I know that by the time rehearsals are over he will not only know what the play is about but will have made a major creative contribution to it.[47]

The preparation of *Search,* a realistic documentary about a U.S. Navy air-sea rescue of fliers forced down at sea, gives some indication of the care and long, hard work that went into a *Philco Playhouse* script. In 1951 Coe decided that he wanted to do a play about a group of men on a raft at sea. He first tried to get television rights to *Kon-Tiki.* Failing this, he next attempted to do a dramatization of Eddie Rickenbacker's *Seven Came Through.* He was able to clear the rights, but unable to reach the seven survivors featured in the book for personal clearance, as they were then scattered all over the world. Coe then approached writer David Shaw with his idea and hired him to write a documentary play on air-sea rescue. Then followed a series of trips to the Navy Department in Washington. Coe and Shaw went together, and at times separately, to speak to Naval experts, to question airmen returned from Korea, and to screen film for possible use in the production. Then the script was written and forwarded to Washington for final approval. Delbert Mann was assigned as director and joined Coe and Shaw in further trips to Washington to screen additional film. The final production included 35 brief film sequences.[48]

The Great Kraft Theater

The Kraft-sponsored show continued its prominent role and the J. Walter Thompson Agency was as outstanding and influential as ever. It deserves much of the credit for introducing another new writer, Rod Serling, through the medium of its half-hour *Lux* show and hourly *Kraft Theater.* Mr. Serling gave most of the credit for his rise to fame to the *Lux Video* show, stating that over a two-year period (1951–1953) they bought 12 of his shows and produced 11 of them. (The *Lux*

Video Theater had been a second effort of the J. Walter Thompson Agency, after the big success of the *Kraft Television Theater.*) Serling cited specifically Dick McDonagh, a script editor of the J. Walter Thompson Agency, who "gave me many moments and several words of encouragement and enough pats on the back to keep me propelled forward."[49] The *Lux* show eventually became an hourly drama and moved to Hollywood where the new producers used old movie scripts. It had earlier been cited by Gould as "one of the better half-hour programs devoted to original drama."[50] Serling gave his reaction in describing the work of the show before it changed hands:

> In its New York half-hour days, the *Lux Video Theater* proved itself symptomatic of the basic difference between what was Hollywood television and what was then New York City television. It was a show that consistently aimed high. Its whole conception in terms of dialogue and production was adult, never hackneyed, and almost always honest. It touched upon themes like dope and marital infidelity. It did things like adaptations of short stories by Faulkner and Benet. It encouraged the submission of original scripts by any writer who knew how to write, regardless of what his credits were.[51]

The first of the Faulkner stories that Serling mentioned was produced in April of that season. It was *The Brooch,* and was badly panned by the critics. Gould in the *Times* described Faulkner as "the latest victim of TV's taboos." The play, as presented on television, "was the story of a comparatively innocuous and uncomplicated juvenile who overrides his mother's wishes and marries a sweet young girl...." As written originally, "it was the story of a characterless mama's boy who marries a tramp and commits suicide when she leaves him." Here is an instance where a change in story ending is necessary in order to meet the requirements of the television code which holds that suicide is undesirable as a solution for life's difficulties.[52] *Variety* concurred, describing the adapation as "a saccharine bawdlerization of the literary qualities of the original story."[53] Evidently, Faulkner was undeterred by the failure of this production to receive critical plaudits, for the following season a second Faulkner short story, *Shall Not Perish,* was adapted and produced on the Lux series.[54] It was not reviewed.

As a television dramatist, Rod Serling was quite different from the writers who achieved recognition on the *Philco* show. Though his plays in the next few years capitalized on the intimate, personal nature of the television medium, his characters were set in a larger, more theatrical framework. For example, his two biggest successes in later years and the winners of the Emmy Awards were *Patterns,* a story of a power struggle in big business, and *Requiem for a Heavyweight,* set in the dramatic background of prize fighting. In 1952–53 two of his hour-long dramas produced by the other J. Walter Thompson show, *Kraft Television Theater,* were *The Twilight Rounds,* a prize fight drama, and *Old Mac-Donald Had a Curve,* a comedy about big league baseball.

The Twilight Rounds anticipated Serling's very successful television and film drama, *Requiem for a Heavyweight.* Each tells of a prize fighter who is in danger of being seriously hurt if he engages in another bout. In the latter play the hero retires and seeks to find himself in a world that is unfamiliar and foreign to him.[55] In the earlier play the fighter is urged by his manager to retire, but he takes the advice of his girl friend, who convinces him that he is as good a fighter as ever, and goes on to disaster.[56] These stories were the result of Serling's experience as an amateur fighter in the paratroopers and show a working knowledge of that profession.[57]

The second show, *Old MacDonald Had a Curve,* was one of three comedies Serling wrote up to 1957 in an output of about a hundred scripts, which gives some indication of the small percentage of comedy in live television drama.[58] None of the well-known television writers of this period are noted for writing a comedy drama. This is largely because of the difficulties presented by the lack of a live audience during the television performance and the inability to dub in laughter as in the filmed situation comedies of Hollywood.

Serling stated *Old MacDonald Had a Curve* "was one of the few things I attempted with nothing but sheer entertainment in mind. I had no axe to grind and no issue to solve."[59] It was a great success. *Variety* said it was "one of the most diverting plays in the now enormous catalogue of the series."[60] The fantastic story concerns an aged pitcher who, as a resident of an old folks home, has as his major activity pitching horseshoes. One day he throws his arm out of joint and develops a freak curve ball. As a result he is signed up by his old major league team in order to pull them out of a long losing streak.[61]

In celebration of its sixth anniversary that season *Kraft* presented four scenes selected from dramas that were among the most outstanding in its history: *Wuthering Heights, Of Famous Memory, January Thaw,* and *My Brother's Keeper.* The newspapers said they were selected on the basis of audience opinion and explained no further.

Rice could not remember any details but suggested availability of actors was probably an important consideration.[62] After the performance *Kraft* held a "Come As You Were" ball at the Waldorf Astoria for 500 of its former actors and actresses and paid the Eaves Costume Company to costume them in the parts they had played on the *Kraft Theater.*[63] Up to that time the *Kraft Television Theater* had presented 22 classics, 169 Broadway adaptations, 23 adaptations from the London stage, and 40 original television dramas![64]

Robert Montgomery Presents

The *Robert Montgomery Show* on NBC was gradually receiving more recognition in the television industry. With Norman Felton and Herbert Swope, Jr., as the directors, its adaptations in 1952–53 won it the "Best Dramatic Show" in the fifth annual Emmy Awards of the Academy of Television Arts and Sciences, the "Dramatic Show of the Year" designation in the *Radio-TV Daily* annual poll, and the "Best Dramatic Series" title in the annual Sylvania Television awards.

The award situation was still somewhat confused as there was a set of Academy Awards (Emmys) announced on the West Coast and another set of Academy Awards (Michaels) being issued in New York. The New York Michaels Awards' last season was 1952–53 and they gave the *Philco Television Playhouse* a Michael for drama.[65]

In a production sense the *Robert Montgomery Show* was compared with *Studio One* in its high period. Montgomery himself was never available for comment, but certainly the reviews indicated that Felton and Swope deserved much of the credit for the show's continued success. One anonymous source claimed Montgomery never functioned as a real producer but only lent his prestige and occasionally his acting abilities to the series, and that Joseph Bailey, production supervisor, was the show's top executive. The series' most exciting production that season and Montgomery's most successful performance was a version of John O'Hara's *Appointment in Samarra*. Montgomery's performance as Julian English was described as a *tour de force* and the adaptation as "a superb work of enlightened craftsmanship, a drama of integrity and maturity." This is particularly unusual in that, unlike *Lux*'s Faulkner play, the ending was not changed to satisfy the Television Code and the climactic suicide resolved the plot as it did in the novel.[66] The book is loaded with themes that television normally avoided in those days, such as drunkenness, but the play did not shy away from them, and there was no voiced protest, only positive affirmation of a job well done.

The Hallmark Hall of Fame

The distinguished *Hallmark* dramatic show would long outlive the other series dramas and its name would be associated with Franklin Schaefer. But it was Albert McCleery who played the most significant role in its development. It began rather humbly as a half-hour show on NBC in 1951. In 1952–53 it took on a slightly new format and there were intimations of the greatness to come. Sarah Churchill remained as the hostess and Albert McCleery became the producer-director. McCleery brought in an arena style of staging that he had had success with in 1949 in a production of *Romeo and Juliet* for NBC and in a series called *Cameo Theater,* although his settings had become more elaborate as his budget increased.

What was significant about *Hallmark* that season was the occasion of the historic Maurice Evans two-hour television version of *Hamlet.* This television triumph was outstanding in all possible ways. It marked the beginning of the change of the *Hallmark Hall of Fame* format and the development of the respected *Hallmark* tradition in television drama. It signalled the start of Mildred Freed Alberg's career as a producer, and stage director George Schaefer's brilliant career in television. It was yet another high point in the illustrious career of Albert McCleery—with many more to come. It was the television debut of Maurice Evans and was followed by two more, highly praised two-hour Shakespearean productions—*Richard II* in January 1954 and *Macbeth,* costarring Judith Anderson with Evans, in November 1954.

In 1955–56, Mr. Evans produced the series which was known as *Maurice Evans Presents* on the *Hallmark Hall of Fame,* and he was seen in Shaw's *The Devil's Disciple* and in Shakespeare's *The Taming of the Shrew.* In 1956 he starred in Shaw's *Man and Superman,* and Shakespeare's *Twelfth Night,* and he videotaped a production of Shakespeare's *Tempest* which was presented by *Hall of Fame* in the spring of 1960.

The *Hamlet* production was an all time high in the number of producers, directors, sponsors, and network executives who nervously awaited its outcome. The very nature of its two-hour format, the great expense involved, and the universal prestige of its star performer, commanded public and professional interest across the nation. Many a producer undoubtedly pointed to its success when justifying "art" to a budget-minded sponsor, but many a producer doubted its outcome and the value of such an undertaking. After the show signed off, the switchboard at NBC was inundated with calls, and they continued for several days. Evans' mailbox overflowed for days thereafter.[67] The critics hailed it as a stunning production and a great personal triumph of Maurice Evans: "His was a gripping powerful performance," said *Time*.[68] Jack Gould stated, "The tragedy was played for its sheer dramatic value and proved superbly arresting theatre." He said "the deletions were ideal" and "made for a contemporary briskness and vividness."[69] Flora Schreibner in the *Quarterly of Film, Radio, and Television* wrote of "Television's *Hamlet*" as "an experience belonging uniquely and indigenously to television itself," showing that television has "an aesthetic all its own."[70] R.L. Shayon in *The Saturday Review* was, as usual, intellectually obtuse and wrote his review in a somewhat affected fashion in the form of a letter to William Shakespeare. While he did not come out honestly in favor of the production, and parts of the letter admit of several interpretations, on the whole he seemed pleased with what television had accomplished.[71]

After the telecast Evans told of his experiences in adjusting to the special features of the new medium:

> The consciousness that, in television, some of the viewers are thousands of miles away makes problems for the actor... Al McCleery, NBC executive director, and George Schaefer, my own stage director, had constantly to remind me of the actual proximity of the audience. Although people would be sitting before their sets in all parts of the country, I had to remember that on the screen the distance between their noses and mine would average six feet—not six miles or six hundred.
>
> Accustomed to playing *Hamlet* in the wide spaces of the theatre, I found it excruciatingly difficult to deliver certain passages with the requisite vehemence without looking ridiculous at such close quarters...
>
> In rehearsal, we found the best way to scale the performance down to TV proportion was to have an assistant hold a piece of cardboard before the actors' faces. This represented the exact size of the image which would appear on the screen. This device helped me enormously.[72]

Evans also had some marvelous comments about the general
nature of the television medium:

> Those of us who occasionally sigh for the glories of the theatre of the
> past are forced to admit that, from an actor's standpoint, television is
> at least a comfortable refuge from the insults of a hostile audience.
> Although the simple twist of the dial which utterly obliterates an un-
> welcome performer is far more telling than the critical cabbage, the
> television actor can continue doing his worst in a state of blissful
> ignorance—at least until the mail comes in next day.
>
> Another boon that TV confers upon the actor is the absence of
> coughing during a performance. It is not unusual to see some afflicted
> member of the studio personnel rushing for the neatest exit before he
> commits the greatest professional faux pax—the unsuppressed sneeze.
> Comparing this social nicety with the catarrhal cacophony which greets
> me nightly when I face a "live" audience at *Dial M for Murder,* I am
> bound to admit that in this respect television has its advantages. On the
> other hand, of course, the absence of an audience seems very strange
> at the end of show. Instead of the descent of the final curtain and the
> applause across the footlights, the television actor is required to remain
> motionless until a voice from the control booth says "O.K.—wrap it
> up!"[73]

The *Hamlet* telecast was also a spectacular success for Mildred
Freed Alberg, who had suggested the show and "sold it to NBC." She
eventually became the executive producer of the series.[74] McCleery felt
he had not received credit for "the spadework" he did for this show, and
he was unhesitant in downgrading Alberg's contribution. He gave what
he described as "the true story of *Hamlet*" and told how he flew to Kansas City and sold the idea to Mr. Hall of Hallmark Cards:

> Mildred Alberg's husband had worked with Maurice Evans and she
> asked him [Maurice Evans] if he would like to do *Hamlet* on television.
> She came to NBC and asked them. All she had was Maurice Evans—she
> sold *him.* Jack Rayle called me in and asked if I thought Mr. Hall would
> do it. Fairfax Cohen, the advertising genius behind the Hallmark show,
> suggested I take the idea to a meeting with Mr. Hall. I flew to Kansas
> City and talked for one solid hour to Mr. Hall and sold him. Hall didn't
> quite know who Maurice Evans was and he was hesitant. He went off
> an hour, called Cohen and we were in. I insisted on a two hour produc-
> tion, and he agreed to take half the expense. Schaeffer Pen was going
> to sponsor the second half but backed down and NBC took a $50,000
> loss on the show.[75]

This account agrees with the *Variety* report that NBC sought two
advertisers, each to pay $75,712 for time and talent. However, when no

one could be found to take the risk on "such a highbrow production," Hall "stepped into the breach" with a solo offer of $100,000.[76] McCleery described Hall as a "shrewd and brave" man, but he found it strange that Hall "has had more publicity than other sponsors as an understanding and culturally inclined man." He felt that Hall was one of the "strictest" sponsors he had ever worked with. McCleery spoke further about his work with Evans:

> Maurice Evans was very cooperative. It was Maurice Evans' *Hamlet* and it was my job to shoot the *Hamlet* the way he wanted it. It was my floor plan. We had troubles with the network; we couldn't get the studio we wanted, but it was a smooth, happy, working relationship.[77]

The Celebrity Writers

NBC instigated one other interesting attempt to solve the problem of program materials that received considerable publicity but accomplished very little. In 1952 it signed a contract with Robert E. Sherwood whereby he was to write nine original plays for television. He received wide latitude in subject matter and was promised no sponsor interference.[78] CBS followed up by signing Ben Hecht to a contract whereby he was to write two half-hour plays a month.[79] Also the CBS *Omnibus* series put Maxwell Anderson and William Saroyan under contract. Very little came of these arrangements, but the *Robert Montgomery* show, which continued to produce mostly adaptations and participated only slightly in the great excitement over original television dramas the next three seasons, did open its 1954 season with the second play by Robert Sherwood. The first play under Sherwood's fabulous and highly publicized contract was *The Backbone of America,* and a special performance was presented in December of 1953. It was severely criticized. The second play, *Diary,* was the opening production for the *Robert Montgomery* series and was pictured as "somewhat better than the first" but still "not a stirring or stimulating drama."[80] Even R.L. Shayon, who was obviously loath to criticize the respected Sherwood, made apologies for him and was forced to admit that the show was a "flop."[81] George Rosen in *Variety* also felt that in contrast to Sherwood's previous endeavor, he had "come a long way in adjusting his talents to the newer medium." But he concurred it "still betrayed a crudity."[82] Sherwood evidently resigned himself to failure on television, for NBC announced in February that he was released from his contract. He stated he had asked to be released so that he could devote himself to projects in the motion pictures.[83] He died shortly thereafter.

CBS Presents

CBS was still in there trying in 1952 and 1953 with its *Studio One* and the new *Omnibus* series. Donald David and his wife, Dorothy Mathews, had been coproducers of *Studio One* since Worthington Miner left in April of 1952. *Variety* reported, however, that the show had slipped behind NBC's *Robert Montgomery Presents* which was opposite it on Monday nights, and CBS board chairman William S. Paley and the sponsor were "reportedly unhappy."[84] Gould in the *Times* agreed that *Studio One* "has tended to flounder in rather trite seas." As a result CBS brought in Fletcher Markle, who had produced the first *Studio One* as a radio show, "to restore the program's former luster."[85] Mr. Markle's first attempt was an adaptation of a novel, *I Am Jonathan Schrivener,* and *Variety* said it had "a professional finish that restores the program to its original stature."[86] Markle thereafter completed *Studio One*'s season with a series of adaptations.

In spite of the agitation about film, the individuals involved in live drama showed a sense of purpose and glowed with pride when interviewed about these beginnings. Live drama was not declining. The best was yet to come.

5
1953–54 and 1954–55:
Pat Weaver

The Peak Seasons

Variety suggested in the fall of 1953 that it was the live shows' turn "to garner the headlines" and that television films were "having hard sledding."[1] The "B" moviemakers and independents were still grinding out film but use of film by the networks had fallen off by 12 percent in 1953.[2] The one hour dramatic series would seem to be leading a rather steady life, and color and "spectaculars" were still in their future. Most of the news items at this point were concerned with whether the movie producers would eventually release new feature-length films to television. The major studios were not yet heavily involved in films for television, and for many years, most of those produced were innocuous little half-hour situation comedies. They were all alike, many imitating the highly successful *I Love Lucy*.[3] Another trend discernible that season was Hollywood's rush to buy up television scripts. Among these were *Marty, The Bachelor Party, Patterns, The Rack, Crime in the Streets, 12 Angry Men, Visit to a Small Planet,* and *No Time for Sergeants.* One script, *Operation Home,* was bought for $50,000 even before it was produced on *Studio One.*

Sports programming was not yet a major money maker. It was a long time before *Monday Night Football* would be a factor in prime time programming. News programming was gradually becoming a prestige item for the network producers but was almost an adjunct consideration when network executives looked at budgets and profits.

Perhaps the biggest headlines, and one of the more dramatic uses of television, occurred during the Army-McCarthy hearings from April to June of 1954. For quite a time the television and political commentators failed to see what was happening to Senator McCarthy because of his television exposure; and what would happen to politicians as television began to play a dominant role in our political lives.

For three more seasons networks would budget huge amounts of money and reap huge profits from prime time live series dramas and live variety shows and new series would be attempted in all of those years. ABC was the leader in new production ventures in 1953–54. This smaller network had more investment capital in 1953, having consolidated with Paramount Theatres, Inc. It made one last desperate attempt to compete with the leaders on their own playing fields with three new series, the *U.S. Steel Hour,* the *Motorola Television Hour,* and a second version of *Kraft Television Theater.*

The 1954–55 Season

The 1954–55 season was remarkable in terms of quality; it had everything from *Peter Pan* to *Patterns,* and it had quantity besides. An examination of a sample week March 6–12, 1955, shows that nine hour-long live dramas and three live variety shows were broadcast every week. Included in the live drama in that single week were *Crime in the Streets* by Reginald Rose, a television adaptation of *Billy Budd,* and two 90-minute spectaculars, *Peter Pan* and *The Connecticut Yankee.* That season was live television drama's highest point of development and Ed Sullivan was a national hero. NBC produced three new series of color spectaculars: *Producer's Showcase* and two series of Max Liebman musicals; and CBS began a monthly series entitled *Best of Broadway* and a weekly series, *Climax.* That year the television writer was given more credit and acclaim than ever before. He achieved such status that by September of the following year Worthington Miner asked the Pulitzer Prize committee to establish special recognition for television writing.[4]

More than anything else, however, 1954–55 was the season of NBC's color spectaculars. NBC under the leadership of Pat Weaver held a virtual monopoly on exciting news items with their unprecedented break with broadcasting's tradition of regular programming in favor of special one-shot theatrical events. Repetitious scheduling had been a part of broadcasting philosophy for so long that no one had thought it could be any different.

The NBC Peacock Replaces the RCA Dog

The season 1954–55 was color television's introductory year. The spectacular growth of television had been subjected to equally spectacular growing pains in terms of color. Some of these troubles were caused by FCC regulations, others by the industry's inventiveness which made color systems obsolete almost month to month, and mostly by the fierce competitiveness between CBS and NBC. The FCC had tried to authorize a system of color television early in order to avoid a situation wherein black-and-white television sets would be rendered obsolete. The Commission had examined the color question in 1940, 1945, and 1947. Finally in 1950 it approved the CBS mechanical color system which was "incompatible" — that is, the picture could be received only on color receivers.[5] The television set manufacturers were unhappy with the CBS system. They ignored it, and the Korean war restricted production while NBC perfected its electronic system in which the color pictures could be received in black-and-white over existing sets. In December 1953, the FCC, after renewed consideration, approved NBC's compatible color television, and in 1954–55 NBC launched a major color programming schedule.[6] CBS also began a limited schedule of color telecasting with the NBC system.[7] In all, about 500 telecasts in color were carried that season. Among the plays shown in color were *Heidi, Cyrano de Bergerac, Alice in Wonderland, The Constant Husband, The Caine Mutiny Court Martial,* and *The Devil's Disciple.*[8] Production costs for these color shows averaged 10 percent over black-and-white. At the outset the networks absorbed the entire cost differential between black-and-white and color transmission, since the costs could not be passed on to advertisers until there were enough color receivers. This was not a financial burden on the networks, for the *Broadcasting-Telecasting Yearbook* reported that national advertisers spent $840 million on network advertising in 1955. This made television the number one advertising medium, well ahead of newspapers, which had been traditionally first.[9]

"Spectacular" Pat Weaver

Certainly, of all the events in this strange period of the American arts, the strangest was the elevation in 1953 of Sylvester L. (Pat) Weaver to the presidency of NBC. During this period, Weaver, a rare creative genius, would invoke the most startling changes the broadcast industry had ever seen, and change broadcasting forever. It is unusual that a man of his daring and creativity could rise to the top of a major United States corporation. When the announcement was made, he stated to the press: "Basic to the broadcasting business is the quality and character of its program structure — 'the play's the thing.'"

Pat Weaver, ex-naval commanding officer, ex-advertising executive, ex-producer, director, writer, was a man of considerable accomplishment and had been advancing in the network hierarchy for several years. He had joined NBC in 1949 as vice president in charge of television when CBS's much-publicized talent raid had attracted many top stars to CBS. By its aggressive policies CBS had replaced NBC as the leader in radio and had the major share of successful television shows and personalities. Weaver and his associates rebuilt NBC's television program structure and by the fall of 1950, NBC-TV was fully sponsored from 3:00 p.m. to midnight and had begun to make money. In 1952 as vice chairman of the NBC Board of Directors he led the network in the battle for color. His success was attested to by the FCC's reversing its earlier ruling favorable to CBS color television.[10]

Weaver's leadership was so dynamic, it was bound to be controversial. His method of informing and stimulating his personnel, for example, received considerable publicity because of the long rambling memos he used. One such memo on *Matinee Theater* is included as an appendix to the present volume. Another memo on television drama caused much controversy and discussion in the industry after it was secretly acquired by *Variety* and published in January of 1952, though Weaver had asked that it be kept "within the family." The memo filled eight columns in *Variety* and dominated the industry 'talk' for months. In it Weaver urged his executives and producers to attempt something distinct and important in original television drama. He stated that he was discoursing on the dramatic form for television and its limitations. He rambled on:

> So far, no television original has been a smash, if you take the top
> five or ten to be a smash. Berle works from a vaudeville house, . . .

Godfrey works a radio show... Philco is a legitimate house. Montgomery presents a movie. And so on.

...I grant that we must encourage you from management... I am having studios designed that will make O.B. Hanson cry like a baby and General Munson apply for transfer to Attu as a corporal [Munson was network director of operations and Hanson was in disbursing].

...the stakes for which we are engaged are breathtaking ... courage ... optimism...[11]

Throughout the memo there ran a sense of high creative purpose, of broadcasting's manifest destiny to achieve something significant in the field of original drama. In contrast, *Variety* published three weeks later a "rebuttal" by Hubbell Robinson, Jr., program director for CBS, and later its chairman, which ridiculed Weaver's high-sounding words and high intent. He was very brief and very specific in listing what he dubbed "high water marks in creative achievement in the ten past months" on CBS. Included in the list were *I Love Lucy, See It Now, Ed Sullivan, Arthur Godfrey* and *CBS Television Workshop*. He concluded, "These are the specific thoughts I have—279 words."[12]

How *Variety* acquired the Weaver memo was never disclosed. Even though a busy executive, Weaver was generous in sharing his remembrances, but he was not happy in 1959 when remembering the purloined memo.

One of the most spectacular of Pat Weaver's programming changes was the previously mentioned break with broadcasting's tradition of regular programming. "*Regular* programming built *regular* viewing" was an absolute commandment of broadcasting, as inherited from radio—it was the "holiest of holies" in the world of broadcasting.[13] Repetitious scheduling had been the standard for broadcasting since the beginning and no one dared to think that it could be any different. Pat Weaver said "no" to the lords of the broadcasting industry and pushed NBC into scheduling special one-shot theatrical events. They eventually came to be known as "specials" but in 1954 they were "spectaculars," and there were two series of them produced for NBC by Max Liebman. These 90-minute "spectaculars" were a large part of NBC's highly publicized "year of color."

One series was produced every fourth Sunday and the other every fourth Saturday. Max Liebman had been hired by Pat Weaver as the producer of *Your Show of Shows*, a 90-minute revue for NBC every Saturday night in 1952–53 and 1953–54. This series had been conceived by Pat Weaver as a method of getting top stars on television. Liebman set out his aims as producing "a full fledged musical show" every two weeks for nine months:

> Some of these were to be completely original, some would be revivals. Some would have a book; some would be revues. All of them would be loaded with big names and given lavish productions in television color.[14]

The first of these much heralded color "spectaculars" was *Satins and Spurs,* an original musical comedy by Max Liebman and Billy Friedberg, starring Betty Hutton. The critical reaction was cold. Perhaps they "erred by staking everything on the personality of one star." Betty Hutton "just wasn't funny" and there was "too much addiction to color" said the *Times.*[15] The *Broadcasting-Telecasting* reporter described it as "a smash for Betty Hutton," but only "adequate entertainment."[16] John Crosby in the *New York Herald Tribune* did not like any of it: "Whenever things started running down and they started running down all the time—Miss Hutton sprang up and started shaking like a bowl of jelly...."[17]

Other "spectaculars" produced in the early months of the season were *Lady in the Dark* with Anne Sothern; *The Follies of Susy,* with Jeanmaire; *Fanfare* with Jacques Tati; and *Naughty Marietta* with Patrice Munsel. Critical reaction was favorable most of the time, although it was on the whole somewhat reserved. *Lady in the Dark* was the only "smash" hit. The *Times* described it as "real theater":

> It had vitality, it had mood and it had illusion—all the way from start to finish. This viewer had no idea how rewarding the show was in black-and-white, but color gave a breath-taking beauty. It was remarkable, even to the commercials which did not intrude on the play.[18]

Pat Weaver not only made the decision to break into the regularity of the television schedule, he also provided that these shows would have the largest program budgets in broadcasting history to bring to the screen the highest priced stars and the best scripts. But when at first these programs did not break habitual viewing patterns and did not obtain outstandingly large audiences, *Variety* reported that "everyone was having second thoughts" and "plenty of worries."[19] The Nielsen audience rating figures did place *Lady in the Dark* as one of the ten programs with the most viewers in a two week period, but the producers and sponsors of the other nine pointed out that the sponsor had paid as much as five times the budgets of some of the other popular shows.[20] The trade papers were filled with charges and counter-charges.[21] A large measure of the published critical comment came from Raymond Spector, advertising agency head in charge of the Hazel Bishop account, which had financed two of the "spectaculars." It was charged that these programs were too expensive, and that they would never build large audiences.[22] But NBC continued producing and in February loudly proclaimed that 8 of the first 11 "spectaculars" were in the Nielsen top 10.[23] Nielsen's year-end figures did show that the average rating of the first 28 spectaculars was 40.0. This compares with an average of 32.2 for the hourly dramatic series, and 34.6 for the hourly variety shows.[24]

The controversy over the spectaculars threw Pat Weaver into the spotlight. Robert Lewine, an NBC vice president at that time, commented that this controversy was the beginning of Weaver's downfall, for "big corporations do not like their executives to get too much personal publicity."[25] Lewine worked for the Sarnoffs and was soft-pedaling the issue. The situation has always been exactly the opposite in the mass media. There is every indication that General Sarnoff had always been a center of media attention, and he personally disliked employees taking over the center stage.

By 1955 Weaver was moved off to the side as chairman of the board at NBC and General Sarnoff's son Robert became president. In September of 1956 Weaver resigned. The newspapers said there were "policy differences" with the General. There were rumors of personality clashes but Weaver said a flat "no" to all of it. Perhaps, as Weaver said when describing the *Home Show* to this writer, "The most successful shows fold when they have run their course."[26]

Pat Weaver's ideas and changes have outlasted him and are still proving to be some of television's most successful features. Another of those legacies from radio that had to be overthrown was the conventional sales method of single sponsors for weekly program series. To finance his costly "spectaculars," Weaver introduced the "magazine concept" of advertising which allowed advertisers to get on the air for smaller sums as the show was sold to multiple sponsors on an insertion or participating basis. Weaver talked about how "I conceived these shows and how to sell them. I sold *Show of Shows* in minutes, sections. This let us sell to small advertisers. Of course, NBC's business went through the ceiling and a lot of little people became big people."[27]

Weaver's magazine concept allowed a network, like a magazine, to control its own editorial concept and brought a broader base of advertisers to television. He used this concept to finance a number of the other great shows he created for NBC, significantly, the *Today* and *Tonight* shows which have been smash hits for over thirty years! He also created *Matinee Theater, Home Show,* and applying the same principle to radio, *Monitor.* Weaver commented in 1960 that in all the controversy over his leaving NBC it was "never publicized too well that when I was in charge there was a huge profit. Now it's different and they will never catch CBS and ABC. They've had it."[28] He was exaggerating when bringing up sour memories but was only a little off. NBC caught them, but it took 25 years.

Weaver's aggressive programming might be interpreted as an attempt to gain new revenues and to assume financial leadership of broadcasting from CBS. On the other hand, NBC had always been the leader in dramatic programming, and Weaver's "creative programming" activities had been in operation a number of years.[29] Jack Gould rushed to Weaver's defense, stating he was "fighting a very lonely battle," when the whole trend was to turn television into a "home nickelodeon."[30] Weaver stood by his concepts under the criticism of "low circulation" and "flops":

> We're standing pat. I was never more sure of anything than I am about this, our present strategy.[31]

He acknowledged there would be misses along with hits and commented about ratings:

> And what is so bad about *Lady in the Dark* getting into 10,000,000 U.S. homes! Yet for only a small part of the cost it would have entailed had Oldsmobile taken a full page ad in the nation's dailies for a single insertion. Yet here for the client was taste and a sense of excitement he had never yet experienced.[32]

Weaver was vindicated the next season when CBS followed his lead and produced ten "90-minute spectaculars." The history of television has been more and more "specials" ever since. By 1959 NBC would budget $31 million for specials and CBS would claim to have 200 specials in the 1959–60 line-up, although it never quite reached that figure. In a few years the major hour-long dramas from Hollywood, such as *The Untouchables, The Fugitive, Ben Casey* and *Peyton Place,* would schedule "special" multiple episode stories which eventually made the rounds of European and American movie houses. The show *77 Sunset Strip* went beyond that and did an ambitious five-hour tale entitled "5." Most two-part shows got high ratings, particularly on the night the show was wrapped up. This idea of Pat Weaver's also led to the current highly successful miniseries concept. But even in 1960 a prominent NBC producer still felt compelled to explain "viewers don't resent irregular programming." Sounds like an old Pat Weaver memo.

A few seasons after the original "spectaculars" the name was changed to "special." Max Liebman, the original producer, commented on this change and blamed this word for part of their troubles:

> But it was almost inevitable the word ["spectacular"] should be taken as a boast on our part, the kind of boast which could scarcely be lived down by even the best of productions.[33]

The great word controversy was second only to the controversy that surrounded Weaver's resignation. Weaver had his own fascinating comments:

> Max didn't like the word but he didn't know what he was talking about. Max called them Specials from the beginning. I picked the name. The idea of the Spectacular came about for a number of reasons but mostly the comedy shows, *Colgate Comedy Hour,* the *Show of Shows, All Star Revue.* These shows were the basis for it.
>
> Continuity, frequency, consistency were inviolate rules of programming. I said we don't need them. Spectacular was a form of programming that would preempt time so you could do whatever you wanted. It was the year of color.
>
> There were a number of different reasons. A number of great artists wouldn't work in television. They needed money, publicity, a special event. Another reason was a number of advertisers had special purposes they wanted to achieve that regular shows couldn't. In spite of the variety, we already had a time problem. We were handcuffed by regular programming.
>
> As usual with an innovation, the people who don't want change, picked the few flops and raised hell. *You always have flops in show business!* [That's the way he said it, italicized, with an exclamation point, waving his hands!] But all the advertisers renewed; all found it was effective in selling.
>
> Max Liebman just didn't know. He's not an ad man. They took a visceral connotation of the word and twisted it. It's a good word in the ad business and it sold an idea to the agencies![34]

Part two of "operation spectacular" at NBC occurred the following season, 1954–55. It was the monthly 90-minute *Producer's Showcase,* which specialized in straight drama on an elaborate basis. It was not as much a focal point of fanfare and publicity as were Max Liebman's musicals, but was a tremendous prestige presentation in the sense of *Celanese Theater*. It lasted two years, and in the end its value to the network was questioned, just as *Celanese Theater* had been questioned, because it failed to achieve high ratings in comparison with high costs. Fred Coe was the producer, with Delbert Mann and Arthur Penn continuing as his directors, and Showcase Productions, a package producing organization of Henry and Paul Jaffe, was the producing organization.

The origins of Showcase Productions, which in October 1955 took over production of the *Alcoa-Goodyear Playhouse,* was much like that of Talent Associates. Henry and Paul Jaffe were lawyers handling theatrical clients just as David Suskind had been. One of their clients, Leland Hayward, had the idea of producing a monthly 90-minute show. Weaver was receptive to this idea as part of his color programming, but Heyward became ill and Fred Coe was brought in to replace him. The Jaffes stood by as legal watchmen over the company they had created for Heyward, and *Producer's Showcase* was born.[35]

The initial presentation was Noel Coward's *Tonight at 8:30* which was described as "a personal triumph for Ginger Rogers."[36] It was followed by the Lindsay-Crouse creation of the 1940s, *State of the Union.* Lindsay and Crouse themselves had "modernized" the script, substituting Eisenhower for Truman and freshening it with recent political quips.[37]

And so it went until the climax in March 1954 of what was probably the most successful single show in the history of television. About 65 million viewers saw Mary Martin in a two-hour Broadway musical comedy version of Sir James M. Barrie's *Peter Pan.*[38] After closing, the Broadway production was moved almost intact to television with Fred Coe taking over the production reins. More than anything else the show was a great personal triumph for the celebrated actress, Mary Martin. The reviewers outdid themselves with praise. A clipping folder in the NBC files contained 23 separate columns which appeared in newspapers and magazines across the country. Jack Gould said: "Surely there must be a trace of fairy dust from coast to coast this morning,"[39] and George Rosen headlined it, "A Major Television Triumph."[40] The show was repeated the next season, and it won the Emmy award as the best single program and the Sylvania award as the television show of the year.

Certainly, this was just another of the many vindications of Pat Weaver. What did he think were his failures when reflecting a few years later:

> The information programs. When I left we hadn't won the battle to get these on the air. Long power struggles are necessary to pre-empt the time and we needed a balance between public affairs and entertainment. They are doing a good job now.[41]

Pat Weaver was relaxed and amused as he made his epitaph for NBC:

> I ran NBC for 8 years. I used monopoly tactics. I never made any bones about it. I was making a huge profit for NBC so anything came along that looked good I grabbed it. They should never have let ABC get Disney. Or a Miner, a Goldberg. I hired Worthington Miner and never used him. I would never have let ABC succeed. The General is nuts—he's publicity mad. Bobby (Sarnoff, Jr.) is a fool. He fired a man when I was away who had 32 years—and never gave him a pension. He should run a delicatessen and not a good one.[42]

Robert Sarnoff, Jr.'s office pointed out three times that he was too busy to be interviewed. The man Bobby fired, however, was identified by Albert McCleery as an "old henchman to Pat" and an honored name in television history: "He was fired to antagonize Weaver."

Pat Weaver could only have happened to television in the beginning, when it was new—although it resisted him, opposed his changes and eventually rejected him. In the end, people make the difference, not better technology, better facilities, better budgets. And he represented the people television needed.

6
1953–54 and 1954–55: Fred Coe

Philco-Goodyear, the Sixth and Seventh Seasons

The *Philco-Goodyear Playhouse* moved into a magnificent sixth and seventh season. Only the *Kraft Theater* would exceed them. The 1953–54 season was the last in which Fred Coe's full attention was devoted to *Philco Playhouse*. In the fall of 1954, he was assigned to *Producer's Showcase* and his status with *Philco Playhouse* became that of executive producer with several producers working under him.

That season the George Foster Peabody Award recognized the *Philco Playhouse* for "outstanding entertainment," and cited Fred Coe as "the most consistent producer of fine television drama." It especially commended him "for his firm emphasis on good writing."[1] Fred Coe had received a number of other awards. Among these was the annual *Look Magazine* award as "the individual who organized and most creatively presented a television series," which he received for two years; the *Variety* Showmanship award; the Sylvania award for *Marty;* and several Emmys.[2]

In Fred Coe's writing group that season Tad Mosel had his most successful year. Although the production of his *Other People's Houses* on August 30, 1953, was at the tail-end of the 1952–53 season, it seems more appropriate to view it as the beginning of the next season. This was the second of Mosel's plays produced by David Suskind, and it is one of Mosel's better known works. The *Variety* review stated that Eileen Heckart played the part of Inez as if it had been written for her.[3]

Mosel said he cherishes this review "because it indicates that an actress, a director, and a writer worked so closely together and so much to the same purpose that the end result appeared to be a single creative effort." Actually, he stated, the play was written for the "exact opposite" of the tall, angular actress: "I had pictured Inez as motherly, round, soft-voiced, and about fifty years of age." The producer, Suskind, suggested Heckart, and although it had seemed "farfetched" to Mosel at the time, he felt she "gave one of the most rewarding performances I have ever seen in one of my plays."[4]

It was also the beginning of a "rewarding" relationship; Mosel worked with Heckart a number of times, notably in *The Haven,* which he wrote for her. This first play with Heckart, *Other People's Houses,* was a drama concerning old age — as the title so dramatically indicates. The central character, played by Heckart, is "a woman who has been kind all her life and who is suddenly forced by circumstances to do an extremely unkind deed." She is a spinster housekeeper who must put her trusting father into an old man's home because he is childish and irascible and refuses to adjust to living with his son-in-law.[5]

In discussing *The Haven,* which was produced on November 1, 1953, Mosel told "how eventually the play came into the hands of producer Fred Coe, . . . and there began the most important relationship in my life as a writer." Mosel describes this play as "the most popular unproduced play in television history." It was the first play to excite interest in Mosel's work as it passed around from producer to producer, but because of its subject, marital infidelity, and a suicide that occurs before the play opens, he had some difficulty selling it until Fred Coe agreed to produce it.[6] Although marital infidelity and suicide sound like mild stuff today, Mosel related an anecdote that shows some of the ridiculousness of television's early self-imposed censorship. The producing unit had waited many days to hear from NBC's Continuity Department to see if the play would be approved. With the first rehearsal imminent, Delbert Mann, the director, had called the Continuity Department head:

> There was a long silence at his [Mann's] end of the telephone. I had visions of my "immoral" play's being rejected yet again, and this time irrevocably. He finally hung up and admitted that we did have a problem. In the first act there was a reference to an "old Chevy," and since this constituted a rather gratuitous plug for Chevrolet, would we mind changing it to "old crate"?[7]

Rod Serling wrote of a similar experience on a program called *Appointment with Adventure* when he was asked not to use the words "American" or "lucky," because they connotated a rival brand of cigarettes to the sponsor of the program. The words were to be changed to "U.S." and "fortunate." At first Serling was not sure, but after establishing that his "leg wasn't being pulled," he had his name withheld from the script as a protest.[8]

Two of Paddy Chayefsky's scripts that were produced by *Philco* that season were *The Bachelor Party* and *The Mother*. In the first, Charlie, a $75-a-week accountant has just been told by his wife she is pregnant. He is depressed because of money problems and a job that holds no real future for him. To cheer him, his wife encourages him to attend a bachelor party. His depression mounts throughout the party, but in the end he discovers that his life has meaning through his marriage and that marriage is far more than a habit formed by coexistence. *Variety* described it as "a mature script" and a "resounding hit," and gave the credit to Chayefsky.[9] Chayefsky, on the other hand, felt the credit belonged to Delbert Mann, the director. In giving Mann credit, Chayefsky first went into a lengthy description of the "complex and frightening job" of the television director. Then he explained:

> I am not sure to this day where the basic approach was wrong; but obviously the line of the story is six inches off from beginning to end, and the third act resolution is hardly an inevitable outgrowth of the preceding two acts... I wanted to show the emptiness of an evening about town, and emptiness is one of the most difficult of all qualities to dramatize. What Delbert Mann, the director, did was to balance each scene deliberately so that the emptiness became heavier and heavier. The [last] act still required some line relating to the other two acts, and we decided the line that the first act indicated was the leading character's desire to go to bed with a woman other than his wife. It is impossible to write such blatant adultery in a television script.... It was up to the director and the actor to convey this basic thought to the audience. It was done with simple stage business and by a quality in the acting.[10]

Chayefsky's second script, *The Mother,* caused this question to be asked by Patricia O'Connor in a textbook type of analysis of selected television dramas:

> There is a wide, and some say unbreachable, gulf between a king of Greece and a Bronx seamstress [the mother]. The seamstress, they

would say, is about the most uneventful figure in existence, so why or
how write drama about an uneventful woman?[11]

A Chayefsky answer to this question might be selected from his discussion of *Marty:*

> There is far more exciting drama in the reasons why a man gets mar-
> ried than in why he murders someone. The man who is unhappy in his
> job, the wife who thinks of a lover, the girl who wants to get into televi-
> sion, your father, mother, sister, brothers, cousins, friends — all these
> are better subjects for drama than Iago. . . . These are the substances of
> good television drama; and the deeper you probe into and examine the
> twisted semiformed complexes of emotional entanglements, the more
> exciting your writing becomes.[12]

The Mother reveals such probings into the emotional problem of an old
woman whose husband has just died. She craves her independence and
work will give her this, plus the salvation of her integrity as a person.
Her younger daughter has a driving compulsion to win her mother's
love and keep her dependent at home, but the old woman manages to
get a job as a seamstress. She makes a silly error on her first day,
however, and is fired. She resigns herself to living with her daughter,
but after sitting up all night in the strange apartment, it is beautiful
and very moving that she goes out again to try and find a job.[13]

Fred Coe

In the seventh season, 1954–55, the *Philco Playhouse* returned
with Gordon Duff as the producer and Fred Coe as the executive producer, and the Goodyear Tire Company as the alternate week sponsor.
Several new writers were featured on the *Playhouse* that season and the
old series was as successful as ever. One such writer was J.P. Miller, who
came to attention with *The Rabbit Trap,* after which he immediately
left for Hollywood to do a screenplay of the show for Hecht-Lancaster
Productions, as Hollywood increasingly began to lure away television's
writers.[14]

Miller was characteristic of the *Playhouse* writers. Criticized at that
time for being too preoccupied with depressing "slices of Life," *The
Rabbit Trap* was certainly that type of play.[15] It is the story of a draftsman, a sad little man, and his effort to fight his way out of a

personal psychological snare. After being at the beck and call of his employer for years, he finally finds the strength to quit and "call his soul his own." The incident that precipitates the crisis occurs on a vacation in which the draftsman and his son set a trap to catch a rabbit. When the father's vacation is interrupted by the employer, the family hurriedly leaves, forgetting the trap. His son is apprehensive that the rabbit might starve in the trap and this poses a personal challenge to the father when his employer refuses to let him go back and check the trap. The symbolism seems contrived in a summary but the play worked.[16]

Robert Alan Aurthur and Gore Vidal were two other *Philco* playwrights who received recognition that season. Robert Alan Aurthur's *Man on a Mountain Top* won the Sylvania award as the "finest original teleplay of the year."[17] It was set in a Greenwich Village coldwater flat and told of a child prodigy, now an adult genius, who had retreated from life because of lack of love. He feels he is a machine and his psychiatrist father has "left out love" when creating him. In the conclusion it is indicated he will make an attempt to adjust through the influence of a woman.[18]

Gore Vidal was unusual in that he came to television as a successful novelist. The adaptation of his television play, *Visit to a Small Planet,* had a long, successful run on Broadway. Cyril Ritchard starred in both productions. Kreton, a gentleman from another dimension, lands his flying saucer in the backyard of a news commentator. He is fascinated by the helpless earth people and has the power to know what they are thinking. He explains that they will not be civilized for another thousand years and will thrive on violence and savagery. But he is delighted with them and toys with the idea of restaging the Civil War so that this time the South wins. He decides to start a new war to keep Earth people happy, but another saucer arrives in time and he is carted off.[19] Again and again television is too timid. The producers of three series were unwilling to do this show but because of the broad social commentary outlined above, only the *Philco Playhouse* could get its sponsor to agree to the production, even though it was a very light comedy. Vidal, himself, seemed delighted that sponsors took his play too seriously: "The dramatic art is particularly satisfying for any writer with a polemical bent and I am at heart a propagandist . . . complacently positive that there is no human problem which could not be solved if people would simply do as I advise."[20]

Tad Mosel and Paddy Chayefsky continued to write for *Philco.*

Mosel did another play especially for Eileen Heckart, *My Lost Saints,* and by this time Chayefsky had done 12 scripts for *Philco.* Two of his plays that attracted attention that year were *Catch My Boys on Sunday* and *The Catered Affair.* These writers had begun to expand their activities into motion pictures and the legitimate theater, as well as into other series; Mosel, for example, wrote plays for nearly all the dramatic programs on television.

All of these early 1950s seasons demonstrate Fred Coe's great contribution to the television medium in the areas of writing and direction. The artists that he uncovered and nurtured were among television's most talented and productive, and continued so in the film and theater. All of the live dramatic series had provided tremendous opportunities for young writers and perhaps never before or never again will the writer be in such demand. But it was Coe who was credited with almost single-handedly giving these writers a solid artistic status in the television industry. When asked how this came about, he explained that he had established what was virtually "a writing stable" by trying to keep a group of about ten writers busy turning out adaptations.[21] His more specific contributions are harder to describe. The producer hires and buys; he creates a series in the sense that others specifically create an individual drama. But he also is an individual creator and contributes specifically in story conferences with the writers and by attending rehearsals and production conferences with the writers and by attending rehearsals and production conferences with the directors. About this key role of the producer, Chayefsky had this to say:

> It is important to the writer to find a producer with talent and authority. You can write the finest literature in the world, but there has to be someone who will buy it from you and who will fight the vast negative elements in television to see that your show gets on. A good producer hires gifted directors, and a good director is as necessary to a successful television drama as is the basic script.[22]

In his book Chayefsky makes the same complaints that Serling does in his book, *Patterns,* about censorship and the treatment accorded the writer in television. But he has this to say about *Philco:* "I enjoy writing television a good deal for personal reasons and because the *Philco-Goodyear Playhouse* allows me to write as well as I care to."[23] About Coe he is more specific:

> When the script is finished, the writer brings it in to the director and the producer. Again script conferences are called, revisions suggested.

The mood of these conferences varies with the personalities involved. In my case, I have been almost childishly dependent upon the reactions of Fred Coe, the producer (at this writing) of the *Playhouse,* Gordon Duff and Bill Nichols, his associates, and Delbert Mann, who usually directs my shows. By the time I have finished my first draft, I have long since lost my perspective and will accept just about any suggestion they make. It must be made clear that these four men are inordinately talented at their jobs. I don't believe there is a better story mind in the business than Fred Coe's.[24]

Since most of Coe's writers and directors were as unabashed in their praise of him as Chayefsky is, it is perhaps through their comments that Coe's significance may be further assessed. Horton Foote had this to say:

I have never had more dignity of treatment as a writer by producers, directors, and actors than during the production of these plays [on *Philco Playhouse*].

I think a great deal of the credit for this goes to the producer, Fred Coe. Coe believes deeply in writers and his belief, in turn, gives the writer a feeling of confidence in himself, his talent, and his craft. The staff around Coe—Delbert Mann, Vincent Donahue, Arthur Penn, Gordon Duff, and Bill Nichols—all reflected and supported this belief.[25]

And Vincent Donahue said:

Despite his enormous knowledge of television and his constantly coming forward to us with good solutions, he has never become the all-seeing or all-knowing arbiter.[26]

And Delbert Mann wrote sentimental reminiscences about his work with Coe:

The wonderful, frantic, frustrating, exciting Philco days . . . the time you threw the sound man out of the studio . . . The Last Tycoon . . . Van Gogh . . . Othello. . . Ah want it quiet in this studio and ah mean quiet . . . High Tor . . . and what was it called—A Matter of Life and Death (!!!) . . . memories that bless and burn, as they say . . . some burn more than others . . . the raft and the problems with Search—Ah'm payin' all this money for this thing and ah want to see how it works. Ah want to see the water. . .

Paddy and Marty and Bachelor Party and The Mother. . . We're over the hump now . . . wonderful and agonizing memories, funny and sad. It's strange how the rough ones fade in time and the good ones remain. . .[27]

And finally Tad Mosel wrote:

> Fred Coe was the first man to raise the writer to a position of impor-
> tance in television, and to a writer he is a combined father, friend,
> buffer, psychiatrist, and newspaper critic.[28]

When asked about these comments Coe replied: "A composite of that
guy would look pretty funny, wouldn't he?" Certainly the picture of
Coe is an overwhelming one. Coe surrounded himself with and commanded the loyalty of a group of talented writers and directors who
created a style of drama that was neither theater nor movies but
definitely was television.

Top: As early as 1947 the Theatre Guild and the American National Theatre and Academy lent respectability to television's attempts to do live series dramas. Here Helen Hayes (second from right) and others are pictured in a 1947 Guild production of *Dinner at Eight. Bottom:* Another Theatre Guild production in 1947 was *The Traitor* with Tyrone Power (center) and Homer W. Fickett (right\ shown here in a script conference). (Photos courtesy of The National Broadcasting Company, Inc.)

Above: Television's first smash hit was Worthington Miner's modern dress version of *Julius Caesar* in Studio One's first season on CBS, 1948–49. Here in the murder scene with the conspirators, clockwise from lower left, Brutus (Robert Keith), Cassius (John O'Shaughnessy), Decius (Joseph Silver), Casca (Vaughan Taylor) and Metellus (Emmett Rogers). Julius Caesar, center, was played by William Post, Jr. (Photo courtesy of The National Broadcasting Company, Inc.)

Opposite: On May 7, 1947, *Double Door* opened the lengthy run of Kraft Television Theater on NBC. This historically important first production was housed in a tiny studio on a side corridor in NBC and broadcast to an audience of less than 40,000. The play had had an extensive run on Broadway in 1933 but the television critics were unhappy with the Kraft version. It was generally agreed, however, that the show was carefully and smoothly produced and Kraft was pleased. The pleasure for Kraft and the eventually huge national audiences, lasted 11½ years. (Photo courtesy of CBS, Inc.)

Top: Studio One began its nine-year career on CBS in November, 1948, with *The Storm*. Margaret Sullivan and John Forsythe starred. *Bottom:* The highlight of Studio One's second season on CBS was *Battleship Bismarck*, starring Charlton Heston (seated left) and Paul Lukas (standing). It was one of the first successful efforts at spectacular physical production. (Photos courtesy of CBS, Inc.)

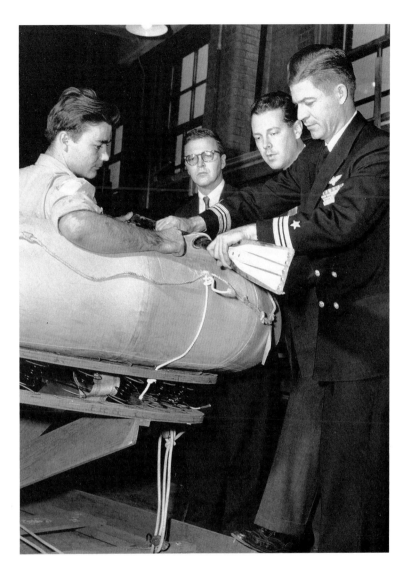

The Search by David Shaw was a realistic documentary about U.S. Navy air-sea rescue. This picture gives some indication of the care and hard work that went into the preparation of a Playhouse original. Bill Shellberger is in the raft; Producer Fred Coe (glasses), director Delbert Mann and Cmdr. Neal, a naval expert, are shown checking the raft device for simulating water action. Coe tried unsuccessfully in 1951 to get the rights to *Kon Tiki* for the NBC Philco-Goodyear Playhouse. He then tried Eddie Rickenbacher's *Seven Came Through* and finally turned to David Shaw to research and write this original drama. The final production used 35 brief film clips. (Photo courtesy of the National Broadcasting Company, Inc.)

Hallmark Hall of Fame began as a live half-hour series on NBC in 1951 and Hallmark is still sponsoring Hall of Fame specials in 1990. The show grew to an hour series in 1952 and in 1953 producer Albert McCleery flew to Kansas City and persuaded Hall to sponsor part of a two-hour version of *Hamlet* with Maurice Evans. The nature of the two-hour format, the tremendous expense and the prestige of the star performer, commanded public and professional interest. It was an outstanding success and Maurice Evans followed with *Richard II* in January 1954 and costarred with Judith Anderson in November, 1954, in *Macbeth* (shown here). They are shown in an NBC publicity photo. (Photo courtesy of the National Broadcasting Company, Inc.)

In 1952 the Philco-Goodyear Playhouse produced *Holiday Song* by Paddy
Chayefsky. He was the first playwright to achieve fame through the television
medium and is most known for his television original *Marty*, which won the
Academy Award as a movie. David Optasha (left), Herbert Berghoff and Joseph
Bulloff starred in *Holiday Song*, the story of a gentle middle-aged cantor who
becomes disillusioned over the misery in the world, especially the anti-semitism,
and eventually regains his faith through an incident on a subway. (Photo courtesy
of the National Broadcasting Company, Inc.)

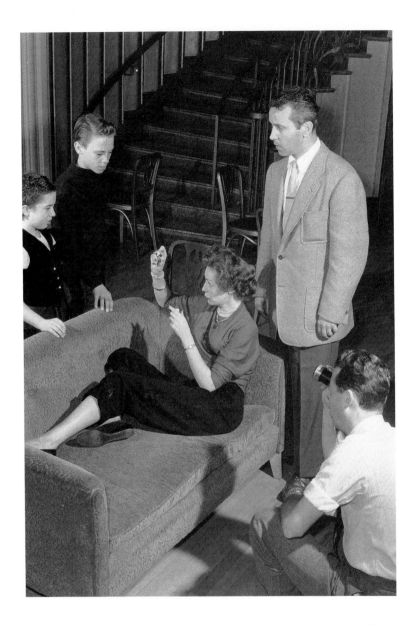

Tad Mosel, one of Fred Coe's "stable" of writers, became enchanted with Eileen Heckhart after her performance in his *Other People's Houses*. She is shown here in *The Haven* on NBC's Philco-Goodyear Playhouse. Mosel wrote the play for her in 1953 and it was rejected by a number of producers because of its subjects, marital infidelity and a suicide that occurs before the play opens, until it finally came into the hands of Coe. (Photo courtesy of the National Broadcasting Company, Inc.)

Top: Playwright Reginald Rose burst onto the CBS Studio One scene in the 1953-54 season with *Thunder on Sycamore Street* starring Kenneth Utt (dark suit) and Nell O'Day (at door). (Photo courtesy of CBS, Inc.) *Bottom:* In 1954 Kraft Television Theater's presentation of Rod Serling's *Patterns* won unanimous praise from the critics and was one of the few live television dramas to be repeated several months later. Ed Begley (left), Everett Sloan and Richard Kiley (standing) starred in this story of a big business power struggle. (Photo courtesy of the National Broadcasting Company, Inc.)

Above: The 1954-55 season on the CBS Studio One was called the Reginald Rose season. It opened with his *12 Angry Men,* a jury room drama that was highly successful as a motion picture, featuring Edward Arnold (standing, left), Franchot Tone, Walter Abel (bow tie), John Beal (hand to chin), Paul Cummings (standing, right). (Photo courtesy of CBS, Inc.)

Opposite: In a bid for "name" writers and top original scripts NBC began contracting well known authors in the early fifties. Robert Sherwood was hired to write a series of original plays for television. He had only a modicum of success and NBC did not renew his contract. Sherwood died shortly afterwards. He is shown on the right in rehearsal for the 1954 *Diary* featuring John Cassavettes (center). The play was featured on the long-running series *Robert Montgomery Presents.* (Photo courtesy of the National Broadcasting Company, Inc.)

Above: Betty Furness was hostess of Studio One for many years and is shown here with Westinghouse flash bulbs. She was known throughout the country for her punch line, "You can be sure, if it's Westinghouse." (Photo courtesy of CBS, Inc.)

Opposite: Playhouse 90 was produced on CBS by Martin Manulis and then Fred Coe. It was an expensive show featuring celebrity stars, quality productions and high ratings. Here Jackie Gleason (right) and director Paul Nickell are examining a set model for *The Show Off.* (Photo courtesy of CBS, Inc.)

Perhaps the most successful single dramatic show in the history of television occurred in 1955 on NBC's Producer's Showcase. The two-hour version of *Peter Pan* featured Mary Martin (laughing at left), with Cyril Ritchard as Captain Hook (right). It received tremendous critical and public acclaim and was repeated live the following year and again in the summer of 1989 from a video tape copy. (Photo courtesy of the National Broadcasting Company, Inc.)

Playhouse 90 on CBS is one of the most remembered of television's live dramas because it survived so long in a live and taped version, well into broadcasting's film era. It was the creation of Hubbell Robinson, Jr., and its second production, Rod Serling's *Requiem for a Heavyweight,* won five of the major Emmy Awards, the first Peabody Award for television scripting and the Sylvania Award as the best play of the year. It was also a highly successful motion picture. This popular photograph shows Keenan (left) and Ed Wynn the only time they appeared together in a drama. Jack Palance is between them as the heavyweight. (Photo courtesy of CBS, Inc.)

Television's <u>first</u> <u>10</u>-year-<u>old</u>!

Now in its 11th year, Kraft Theater has been on television longer than any other show.

It has produced more than 520 hour-long dramas.

Last year it gained a bigger audience than any year in its history and now is seen by about 20 million people a week.

Last year, it produced more *big* shows—sold more scripts to the film industry than any year in its history.

Television's first 10-year-old was the first commercial network show... the first weekly drama show to go on a color schedule.

It has presented such widely acknowledged television masterpieces as "A Night To Remember," "Patterns," "A Profile in Courage." It can make a new star overnight, as it did this year with "The Singin' Idol."

Kraft Television Theater productions are selected, cast, directed and otherwise wholly produced by Kraft and the J. Walter Thompson Company.

If you would like to discuss any aspect of television as an advertising medium, get in touch with the J. Walter Thompson Company office nearest you — or write: 420 Lexington Avenue, New York 17, N.Y.

J. WALTER THOMPSON COMPANY
New York, Chicago, Detroit, San Francisco, Los Angeles, Hollywood, Washington, D. C., Miami and principal international markets.

This advertisement was run in 1957 and features the large blocked "K" and the accompanying toy-sized cameraman, the famous trademark of Kraft Television Theater on NBC. It was introduced by producer Stanley Quinn with *Double Door,* the first show of the 11½ year run of television's longest live series. Kraft Television Theater was a pleasant Wednesday night habit for television viewers and was consistently in the top ten of audience surveys. Produced entirely by the J. Walter Thompson Company, it was a remarkable feat for an advertising agency and, as the advertisement indicates, was seen by about 20 million people a week in 1957. (Photo courtesy of JWT Archives, Manuscript Dept., Duke University Library.)

7
1953–54 and 1954–55:
Kraft, Hallmark
and U.S. Steel

The Kraft Television Theater,
Seventh and Eighth Seasons

Under the sterling leadership of the J. Walter Thompson company the great Kraft Foods Company opened a second *Kraft Television Theater* on ABC in the fall of 1953. This was a major departure in programming economics and format. After six years of success with the NBC *Kraft Television Theater,* the Kraft Company had redoubled its efforts. *Variety* estimated they would spend $6 million a year for the two shows.[1] Edmund Rice explained what happened:

> *Kraft Theater* was extremely successful for the Kraft Company. The products were selling. The ratings were up. There were several strong indications. A cheese product, Deluxe Slices, had been returned in stores with customers complaining it wasn't sliced. We showed how the slices could be peeled off and they never had any more trouble. Television is good for food advertising. They credited television with doing the job for them. But there wasn't enough time on one show for all of their products. The different products in Kraft were fighting over the time allotted, so it was decided to put another show on the air. The first thing we suggested was a different type of show. The sponsor wanted the same kind of thing. They said it was hitting the right kind of audience.[2]

The two plays a week, 52 weeks a year, made for a tremendous job of casting and producing by the J. Walter Thompson Agency. Rice, for example, at various times edited plays for both of these shows plus the *Lux Video Theater*.[3] The Kraft Company, however, ended this unique operation in January of the following 1954–55 season. This was not the end of the series, for another sponsor, Pond's Incorporated, picked up the costs, and it became *Pond's Television Theater,* which continued producing plays through the following summer.[4] According to Rice the reason for the change lay mostly in the small size of the ABC network, which meant "It was not doing well in the ratings."[5]

The original *Kraft Television Theater* on NBC had a relatively unhappy season in 1953–54. Its two biggest years were still ahead — the 1954–55 and 1955–56 seasons. Two serious blunders in the 1953–54 season were its seventh anniversary production, *Alice in Wonderland,* and a one-hour version of *Romeo and Juliet.* The critics were infuriated with the *Alice in Wonderland* production. Jack Gould stated the "treasured story" was "not merely adapted" but "shockingly dese-crated." Its whole spirit, he said, "was violated and largely changed into a coarse, wisecracking charade." Gould complained further that "in an incredible lapse of judgment" Alice was accompanied to Wonderland by Edgar Bergen, Charlie McCarthy, and Mortimer Snerd. "Their often earthy gags and vaudeville quips" were "both outrageous and offen-sive."[6]

On the following Sunday Gould continued to rail at the program: "Rarely in this reviewer's experience has there been such articulate resentment on the part of so many viewers over the treatment of one program [there were many letters to the newspaper]. What made the shock greater was that it came from such an utterly unexpected source. Kraft's standards have always been the best."[7] This writer agrees that he has a strong remembrance of pain when recalling this strange production.

The *Romeo and Juliet* production starred 16-year-old Susan Strasberg, the daughter of Lee Strasberg, the noted director. She played Juliet, a role written for a 14-year-old girl. The NBC press department made much of Strasberg's youth, but *Variety* said "she lacked the maturity to get the full meaning of the part across." Shakespeare had been doing quite well on television but this production "missed the boat in almost every department," chiefly in "the 60-minute digest limit," which was "a tough hurdle."[8]

In 1954–55 *Kraft Television Theater* came back after the humiliating criticism of its anniversary production the year before, and in that season of "spectacular" adaptations produced the season's most exciting original play. The television industry got very excited about *Kraft's* presentation of Rod Serling's *Patterns;* it won virtually unanimous praise from critics and public, and it was one of the few live television dramas to be repeated intact a month later.[9] It won the Emmy award as the best original teleplay and the Sylvania award as the best dramatic show.[10]

Rod Serling gave Fielder Cook's production the credit, citing the *Time* magazine review that stated it was a soundly built play that had had the most uniquely consistent acting and production ever accorded a television play. Serling said:

> Fielder Cook's direction was creatively and artistically a total triumph; the acting . . . was almost unbelievably excellent.
> The success of *Patterns* was uniquely due to a kind of team effort. . . .
> A totally new conception of the ending came from the editor, Arthur Singer, and it proved to be perhaps one of the most successful and lauded moments of the play. Most television productions are collaborative, but *Patterns* evolved, I think, a little more collaboratively than most.[11]

Serling describes it as "a story of power" that he presented "in terms of big business because there is an innate kind of romance in the big, the blustering, and the successful." It deals with three men: The head of a firm, named Ramsey, who is fanatically dedicated to the growth and expansion of his company; his chief vice president, an older man who is dedicated to the business but whose perspective is influenced by human values; and an ambitious yet sensitive young executive who is brought into the company to supplant the older vice president. Ramsey sets out to force the vice president to resign, and the young executive goes along with his brutal methods until the older man is pushed too far and drops dead at a conference. In the climactic scene the young man confronts Ramsey, but Ramsey challenges him to stay and help make the business grow. The young man does not play the martyr and quit, but stays to take the dead man's place.[12] Most of the reviewers compared it with the highly publicized movie *Executive Suite,* that was playing at that time.

Gould found it "one of those inspired moments that make theater the wonder that it is," and stated:

By comparison, *Executive Suite* might be *Babes in Toyland* without
a score. For sheer power of narrative forcefulness of characterization,
and brilliant climax, Mr. Serling's work is a creative triumph that can
stand on its own.[13]

Time said "the play had areas that made *Executive Suite* look like *Little
Women,*"[14] and Chandler in *Variety* described *Executive Suite* as "a
pale cliché next to *Patterns.*"[15] John Crosby in the *New York Herald
Tribune* stated "it was one of those rare, almost unique combinations
of fine writing, excellent acting, and workmanlike job of directing and
production."[16]

Several other Kraft originals were interesting and were among the
many television originals being published that season. *A Seacoast in
Bohemia* by Ben Radin, which was first presented by Kraft in 1953, was
repeated in a new performance,[17] and with *Elisha and the Long Knives*
by Dale Wasserman and Jack Balch, was published as one of the "Top
Television Shows of the Air."[18] Perhaps more interesting because it was
the exception rather than the rule, was the Eugene O'Neill kick the J.
Walter Thompson Agency went on in February and March of that
season. It started with a revival of *Emperor Jones* in February that was
greatly criticized.[19] *Ponds Theater,* the J. Walter Thompson show
which had been the *Kraft Television Theater* on ABC, followed up in
March with a highly praised version of *Anna Christie,* and a J. Walter
Thompson film series, *Star Tonight,* presented an O'Neill one-act,
Ile.[20]

The J. Walter Thompson Agency had received considerable
criticism the previous season for its *Alice in Wonderland* debacle. This
year *Variety,* in its Show Management Awards, pointed to "the agency's
courage, independence, and responsibility to the public in its choice of
dramatic material." *Variety* could never be accused of high culture
elitism but they sounded a little like it as they listed *The Emperor
Jones, Anna Christie* and *Patterns.*[21] The facts remain. The J. Walter
Thompson Agency was remarkable and unique in an industry highly
criticized for its ethical and cultural standards.

In addition to this heavy dramatic fare, *Kraft* maintained its
modest entertainment-first posture week in and week out. Wednesday
night was *Kraft* night on the tube in homes and apartments around the
nation. Most of us would not have missed it for the world. The J. Walter
Thompson Agency did a rare piece of business indeed.

"All Hail," Hallmark and Albert McCleery

No live half-hour dramatic series had yet emerged as a "big-time" dramatic show comparable in prestige and audience acceptance with such hour shows as *Studio One* and *Philco*. *Lux Video Theater* and the *Hallmark Hall of Fame* were the two biggest contenders in prime time up to the 1953–54 season. *Variety* commented that both in ratings and from a qualitative standpoint, *Lux* had fallen "far short of the goal."[22] *Hallmark* had had a big success with the Maurice Evans' *Hamlet* special, but it too was receiving little attention. As a result Albert McCleery and Sarah Churchill had little trouble in talking Hall of the Hallmark Company into expanding into an hourly format. The J. Walter Thompson Agency had less success with Lever Brothers. In 1953–54 the sponsors moved *Lux Video* to a new producing unit on the West Coast, and it became the first dramatic show to emanate from CBS Television City. It was still a half-hour series but the sponsors produced several full hour dramas,[23] and by 1954–55 it went on a regular hourly basis with adaptations of old movies.[24]

But it was *Hallmark* that got the attention. It first opened in 1953 as a full blown, one hour dramatic series with Albert McCleery the producer-director. Eventually George Schaefer would be thought of as the preeminent producer-director of *Hallmark*. By 1964 he would have produced or directed 49 out of the 60 presentations of the distinguished *Hallmark* extravaganzas. This was the last show to run live dramas and from 1953 into the 60s it aired quarterly shows such as the brilliant exhibition of the Off Broadway musical, *The Fantasticks,* memorable moments in television theater history such as *Little Moon of Alban* with Julie Harris; Alfred Drake and Celeste Holme in *The Yeoman of the Guard; A Doll's House* starring Julie Harris; *Kiss Me Kate* with the dream cast of Alfred Drake, Patricia Morrison, and Julie Wilson; William Warfield in *The Green Pastures,* and *Victoria Regina* and *Pygmalion* also with Julie Harris.[25]

These *Hallmark* shows were expensive packages with high priced talent and first-class production. It all started when McCleery made it the first NBC hour-long live drama series to originate on the West Coast. When interviewed poolside at the Beverly Hilton about the move to Hollywood, McCleery indicated he did not feel the move West was a factor in the eventual deterioration of prime time television: "Absolutely not! Didn't you know I was a leader in that movement?" He explained that NBC had opened two new studios in Hollywood, and they could not get anyone to go out there and use them because the first director to go out, William Corrigan, "came back and complained so much." So *Hall of Fame* went "on a temporary basis for six weeks and stayed for two years!" McCleery told why he liked the West Coast:

> I was very enthusiastic about working out West. We had facilities, space to move around in, young, enthusiastic crews. (The old ones were working in movies. Here in New York they're in their fifties—we've killed off more of those guys with the pace and tensions of television.) We weren't a slave to the transportation companies as in New York. Also the props, scenery and costumes are better. The costumes on the West coast are the most beautiful in the world. Every costume in New York is old and shabby. You actually get something that Minnie Maddern Fiske wore and has been patched a hundred times since. The props are exquisite out there; we have no prop houses in New York to compare with them; and they can give you almost everything—the original. You ask for a Napoleonic carriage and you get the carriage Napoleon rode in—in top shape.[26]

Hall of Fame hardly ever held to the announced purpose of presenting "real stories of great individuals." The most important deviation was a second two-hour Shakespearean production. The play was *Richard II,* for which McCleery returned to New York and worked again with Maurice Evans. This performance received mixed reviews and was not as spectacular a success as the *Hamlet* of the season before, though it was far more spectacular in production values. Hallmark Cards financed the whole $175,000 in production and time costs. There was "a mammoth studio" replete with 40-foot castle walls, "immense interiors of Westminster Hall," massive baroque designs, and wide, open exterior sets. Instead of creating a sense of spectacle and scope, some reviews felt the scenery "confused" and "cluttered" the scene and "the fakery was distracting."[27] Albert McCleery, however, was pleased with their technical accomplishments and had many humorous insights on the production:

> That year we had all the money we wanted. We built forty foot castle walls and filled the studio with groups of black and white horses—they are very sociable and talk to each other, so we had trouble when we put them on opposite sides of the studio. George Schaefer and I directed it together. They [?] bent over backwards hoping we would fight, but we cooperated. Schaefer is an extraordinary, Christian, talented guy. He is a superb craftsman—close to genius.

I wanted to do it as an elaborate cameo but Maurice Evans insisted on his great palace walls. Some of the critics didn't like the set and shooting through the flame. So what, Maurice Evans takes direction beautifully—an artist who absorbs an idea and is so sensitive to direction. They laughed at me having to "direct" Maurice Evans but he was wonderful. I think the prison scene was the most exciting moment in the play and on television ever.

This play also was the beginning of the legend of the famous McCleery stagehand ghost. Maurice Evans was beginning his famous "And now I am alone" when in back way up the long hall this stagehand comes walking in in work clothes. Then he sees he was on camera. Paralyzed, if he hadn't run around like a frightened doe looking for an escape he wouldn't have distracted.

That SOB has haunted me ever since. First show in California another one walked in. The stagehands stick together and wouldn't tell me who he was. So we think he's a ghost (we studied the film clips?). Ever since that Ghost occasionally wanders on and my crew says, "Here he is again!"[28]

McCleery referred to Schaefer's productions of *Green Pastures* and *Little Moon of Albans* as examples of his genius. He also spoke of his relationship with Maurice Evans:

I fell out with Maurice Evans next year [after *Hamlet*]. He insisted on *Richard II*. I wanted to wait. I felt *Richard II* would be a good color production if we could wait, but he absolutely insisted on doing it then. He had his eye on NBC's big new studio in Brooklyn, but I still believe it would have been an ideal production for color.[29]

About this Maurice Evans had this to say:

When I was asked to do a second Shakespearean production for *Hallmark Hall of Fame*, it was logical that I should pick *King Richard II*. For one thing, this is the play which brought me fame, if not fortune, in the United States and is the classic which I have played the greatest number of times. Familiarity with the part of the "skipping king" is a great asset; the intricacies of the technical aspects of television leave little time for the actor to concentrate on creating a new characterization, whereas if you know a part backwards you can devote your rehearsal time to adjusting to the special problems posed by the medium.

Apart from suiting my own convenience, *King Richard II* has become almost a cause as far as I am concerned. Each time I have revived the play, it has evoked the same kind of ecstatic praise from the critics and the same wonderment that it has been so long neglected in the theatre and the classroom.[30]

This was McCleery's last season with *Hall of Fame*. He stated that Hall disliked his productions of *The Imaginary Invalid* and *Moby Dick*. Then when *Of Time and the River* "got blasted by the critics and Hall disliked it also, that began my 'swan song' with him." *Variety* had treated *Imaginary Invalid* as a dud but it described *Moby Dick* as "a fluid dramatic hour — everything was top-notch." McCleery compared his $35,000 *Moby Dick* with the $2.5 million motion picture of the same book. He did not feel they had a better production — "all they had was a big whale that looked fake."[31]

Maurice Evans third Shakespearean production with *Hallmark* came the following season, *Macbeth*, with Judith Anderson costarring as Lady Macbeth. *Hallmark* was getting its money's worth out of the classics. Their PR man proclaimed:

> We have been extremely pleased with the reception given Mr. Evans' Shakespearean plays. We have received thousands of complimentary letters from viewers and so has Mr. Evans. So many of them asked that we do *Macbeth* next that it seemed a logical choice, especially in view of the great success Mr. Evans and Miss Anderson enjoyed with it in the theater.[32]

George Schaefer again staged the show with Hudson Faussett as the television director that year. The show was as critically successful as the first two and collected an even larger audience.[33]

Thunder on Sycamore Street

There had not been much thunder on or about *Studio One* in its post–Worthington Miner years — and then Reginald Rose came along. With Felix Jackson as the producer and Paul Nickell and Franklin Schaffner alternating as directors *Studio One* had continued in 1953 its "classy" adaptations such as the Orwell novel *1984*, and *Camille*, and the series was regaining its former luster.[34] *Studio One* had had a pioneering nature under Miner and it had had a serious tone to its image. And so when it came their time to turn to original playwrights, Rose was a natural.

Reginald Rose's first television play, *The Bus to Nowhere*, appeared on *Studio One* in 1951. From that time until 1953 he was busy doing adaptations for *Studio One*. Then in 1953–54 he burst forth with

Thunder on Sycamore Street and the following season with *12 Angry Men, Crime in the Streets,* and *An Almanac of Liberty* — two of which were made into movies.[35] Rose was live television drama's controversial social-thesis playwright. His "message" in *Thunder on Sycamore Street* defends the individual family's right to be "different" from its neighbors and protests unthinking conformity that can lead to mob violence. It is the story of an ex-convict who with his family has moved into "a fine old neighborhood" to start his life anew. One of his neighbors organizes the community to force this family to move out. Among the group is Arthur Hayes, who seems to be a weakling, yet is intuitively against mob law.

The story is told in three episodes, each beginning at the same time — a few moments before a march on the ex-convict's home. The television viewer was shown, in turn, the animal-like behavior of the ringleader, the pathetic Hayes, and the desperate determination of the ex-convict to stay put. It reaches a climax that reviewers described as having "virtually a religious poignancy." After stones have been thrown at the ex-convict, making him bleed, the weakling, Hayes, steps forward and says the next stone must be thrown at him. The mob disperses and Hayes turns to his wife, who had previously dominated him, and says: "What are you standing there for? My neighbor's head is bleeding."[36] The story line seems to strain credibility but all of the reviewers found the characters vivid and interesting. The show was a great success.

What was most interesting about this production were Rose's comments about his censorship problems with CBS:

> Originally *Thunder on Sycamore Street* was conceived as the story of a Negro who moves into a white community. This was unpalatable to the networks... I felt that a compromise would weaken the play but I decided to make one anyway... The selection of an ex-convict as the protagonist was the obvious choice, since this could offend no known organized pressure groups.
>
> It was variously felt by viewers with whom I discussed the show that Joseph Blake [the ex-convict] was meant to symbolize a Negro, a Jew, a Catholic, a Puerto Rican, a Japanese or Chinese, etc. This was extremely gratifying to me.[37]

An interesting side note was the casting of Kenny Utt, the *Studio One* stage manager, as the ex-convict. Rose described his performance as "one of the most moving experiences of my life":

I don't think I'll ever forget hearing and seeing Kenny Utt thunder out the lines, "I own this house and God gave me the right to live in it. The man who tries to take it away from me is going to have to climb over a pile of my bones to do it," and then watching him walk off the floor minutes later as the play ended, tears flowing down his cheeks.[38]

The next season, 1954–55, was *the* Reginald Rose season on *Studio One*. CBS had produced two new dramatic series that season, *Climax* and *Best of Broadway,* and at the end of the year lured *U.S. Steel* away from ABC, but the only thing on CBS that was not overshadowed by NBC's spectaculars was Reginald Rose's playwriting. With Felix Jackson still producing and Paul Nickell and Franklin Schaffner still directing, *Studio One* added new laurels to its long history of quality programming. Rose's *12 Angry Men* won the Emmy award as the best dramatic script, and *Variety* cited him with "a special Writer Award" in its annual Show Management Review. Listing "his magnum opus" *12 Angry Men,* plus *12:32 a.m., An Almanac of Liberty,* and *Crime in the Streets* as examples of unusually superior drama, it stated:

> The Rose saga as a man of conscience and integrity was sneaking up the season before. . . . In a business where the blurbs are easy to bounce, Reginald Rose stands out as the conscience of television.[39]

The drama *12 Angry Men* was the season opener for *Studio One*. It also won a Sylvania award for its camera direction and was highly successful as a motion picture.[40] An interesting sidelight is that it was based on an actual experience of the author:

> A month or so before I began the play I sat on the jury of a manslaughter case. . . I thought then that a play taking place entirely within a jury might be an exciting and possibly moving experience for an audience.[41]

The play is rather difficult to read because the jurors are only designated by number. Rose seems rather artificial again as he pits one man against eleven in order to create a conflict that will make his point. The jury has been called in to sit on a murder trial. Juror number eight holds out for an acquittal, and it boils down to a grapple between him and juror number three in an hour of heated debate. Juror number eight is described as "quiet, thoughtful . . . a man of strength tempered with compassion" in comparison to juror number three as "strong, very forceful . . . with a streak of sadism."[42] Everyone agreed the play was "a wallop on all main counts."[43]

Perhaps Rose's scripts seem artificial these days and the plots somewhat contrived, but in retrospect he and *Studio One* must be admired. In 1954 these themes were daring and his plays are obviously a more vigorous type of drama with more apparent plot and a more positive view of humanity than some of the realistic characters that were associated with the *Philco Playhouse.*

Rose, as did the other writers, gave much credit to his directors: "I have met, worked with, and learned a great deal from brilliant, imaginative directors like Franklin Schaffner, Sidney Lumet, and Paul Nickell."[44]

Some Others on CBS

A comparison between the origins of a new CBS show and the early series such as *Kraft* and *Philco* reveals what a tremendous change had come over prime time broadcasting by that time. Variety shows such as the indefatigable Ed Sullivan's would come and go but the big bucks and the big ratings were in story telling, then and now. This was big business, infinitely complex in its organization, and involving months of careful planning. Let us look at the birth of a show:

In the fall of 1953 and the spring of 1954, the hour between 8:30 and 9:30 on CBS on Thursdays was occupied by two half-hour programs. These two programs had an average weekly audience of less than 11,000,000, or only 29.3 percent of the total audience. The sponsors were dissatisfied, and one issued a notice of cancellation in the spring of 1954. Although the situation was crystallized by the cancellation, actual planning of a new program by the CBS program department had begun in March of 1953 in order to utilize CBS's new studios in Television City in Hollywood, and as part of CBS's general program philosophy of competing with the successful shows on NBC. By that time it was evident that the half-hour format was insufficient for live drama, so the program department began preparation of *Climax* as an hourly show, although there was no decision as to what time period the program might fill. Actually, at that period of television's growth, slots in prime time on the networks were at a great premium, as was seen in Worthington Miner's unsuccessful attempts to get a show on the air. So when an opening appeared on Thursday, it was quickly expanded into an hour, and the program department acquired the rights to 13 stories, representing an investment of $40,000; $15,000 was spent reducing eight of these to the form of a first draft of a television script. In this shape, the show was sold by the advertising sales department to the Chrysler Corporation in May 1954. From May until the fall of 1954, the creative preparation was done by the production department and a producer, Martin Manulis, and several directors were hired. Also the CBS Affiliates Division was busy clearing time on CBS stations across the country, and on October 7, 1954, the first program was broadcast.[45] And the results? Raymond Chandler's *The Long Goodbye* got them off to a flying start and *The New York Times* sent this series "right to the head of the class."[46]

The author did a comparison between reviews and ratings. These are not selected reviews but represent almost the total critical comment available for the *Climax* series from *The New York Times*, *Variety*, and *Broadcasting-Telecasting:*

> *Flight 951*—"exceeded the weight allowance for plot."
> *Dr. Jekyll and Mr. Hyde*—"several megacycles away from the Stevenson classic."
> *Sorry, Wrong Number*—"assorted visual gimmicks that were distracting."
> *A Farewell to Arms*—"spiritless."
> The *Climax* series itself—Season's Summary in *Variety:* "A clinker."[47]

Yet public acceptance of *Climax* was in sharp contrast. The Chrysler Corporation was happy and renewed it the next season as its Nielsen ratings reached as high as 40.9. Several times it placed in the top ten in terms of number of viewers.[48]

Curtain Call at ABC, the U.S. Steel Hour

ABC would be the first network to discontinue live series drama. But in 1953 it joined with the Theater Guild and introduced to television the *United States Steel Hour*. This was one of the most exciting and noble experiments in early television. The famed series would soon be lured away by CBS and thereafter ABC would challenge the leaders, NBC and CBS, with filmed Westerns. And ABC would eventually set them both back on their heels. But for now it was competing with live drama from New York.

The *United States Steel Hour* became one of television's most distinguished and long-lived institutions. It is quite disturbing, although certainly understandable, that current media writers and commentators ignore these series dramas so completely. When it presented its last taped story on television almost ten years later, it would truly be the end of the era. It might seem strange to begin with its ending but it should be mentioned that it did not leave the scene with a whimper but with a bang! The play was Sir James M. Barrie's classic, *The Old Lady Shows Her Medals,* and the stars were Alfred Lunt and Lynn Fontanne. The exquisite Fontanne enacted the old charwoman who pretended she had a soldier son and Lunt acted as narrator and described some of the *Steel Hour's* highlights during its decade of production.

And *Steel Hour* also started with a bang! This was the Theater Guild's second attempt to produce live drama on a biweekly basis. The Guild's first attempt had occurred in 1947–48 when they produced six plays on NBC with Edward Sobel as the producer. Alex Segal held the directorial assignment on the new series and resumed where he left off with *Celanese Theater* two seasons before. The premiere, *P.O.W.,* an original by David Davidson, was an inspired opening performance, with Gary Merrill in the leading role.[49] It dealt with the problem of communist brainwashing of G.I.s and was described as a production of superior quality "that would do credit to a Broadway legiter." Only actors "inspired by a play and director, could have performed with such depth of feeling and understanding." Everyone seemed moved and excited about the performance.[50] *Newsweek* commented: "If it can keep up this quality . . . video audiences will have two 60 minute shows of top calibre (the other: *Television Playhouse*)."[51]

This new series and its quality productions attracted a lot of attention. The *U.S. Steel Hour* won the Emmy award as the best dramatic series in its first season and the *Look* award for "the most consistently presented plays of high merit."[52] Among its productions of note was *The Last Notch,* an original by Frank Gilroy, described as "one of the finest Westerns yet done on live television." It was later produced as a motion picture.[53] One production, *Fearful Decision,* was unusual with its theme about kidnapping. It broke the television code which suggests that references to kidnapping of children are improper. An adaptation of *Hedda Gabler* had Tallulah Bankhead's performance severely criticized as "distracting and wanting" and "too concerned with her performance for its own sake." Perhaps Tallulah was too large for the small screen for where there should have been "a sense of forbidding tragedy," there were "flamboyance, the grand gesture, and the toss of the hair."[54] If one has seen Tallulah on the stage or screen, it is not hard to imagine.

The ABC card files contained no more information than the starting and stopping dates of this magnificent achievement, the *U.S. Steel Hour,* and Segal did not reply to a request for an interview.[55] The evidence on hand, however, safely indicates that Segal's talents and organizing genius were a big factor in the series' success, and the fact that he had the backing and prestige of the powerful and experienced Theatre Guild, plus a large budget from the United States Steel Company.

One of the provisions of the *U.S. Steel Hour* entry on ABC was that the network supply a dramatic series of comparable stature to fill the alternate week time slot. ABC chose its old ABC Album production unit headed by Herbert Brodkin and sustained a series known as the *Television Hour* until the Motorola Corporation picked up the sponsorship in December and it became the *Motorola Television Hour.* The series had a moderate success, getting fair ratings but very little attention in contrast to its partner.[56]

The season 1954–55 was *U.S. Steel's* second and last on ABC and was ABC's last attempt to compete with the "big boys" at this level. *No Time for Sergeants* by Mac Hyman and *The Rack* by Rod Serling were the two most interesting productions. *The Rack* told the story of an Army captain charged with collaborating with the enemy in Korea. It was similar to *P.O.W.*, which had premiered the *U.S. Steel Hour* in 1953, and also concerned brainwashing prisoners of war. This one, *The Rack*, was submitted in rough draft to the Theatre Guild as a kind of courtroom drama which posed the problem: "Was it morally right to punish men for breaking under a form of duress which was not physical when they were exposed to an enemy whose frame of moral reference was totally unlike our own?" On the basis of that draft, Serling was given an option payment and asked to go down to Washington and talk to some of the Pentagon personnel. About the show he had this reaction:

> Among the hundred or so television dramas that I have written and produced, *The Rack* holds a number of distinctions. It was nineteen months in creation, which is the most time I have ever given to any single play; it took the most number of rewrites—seven—and when it

was finally produced it was the closest to what I had imagined it would be of any other play I had ever written. Add to these technical distinctions an almost universally favorable audience and critical reaction.[57]

Serling was quite delighted with his play, also describing it as "one of the most honest things I have ever written." He admitted that in his first draft he had found the officer guilty but presented the verdict as basically unjust and incorrect. After talking with the officers at the Pentagon, he attempted to picture the guilty verdict as the correct one.[58]

In a lucky break that season, the producers of U.S. Steel got the television rights to the book *No Time for Sergeants* for $1,500 before Broadway and the motion pictures began to bid for it. Its production was the debut of Andy Griffith, who up to that time had been playing Sir Walter Raleigh in *The Lost Colony* for seven summers at Manteo, North Carolina. Gould described it as "good, rowdy fun."[59]

The alternate week show to the *U.S. Steel Hour* in its second season was called the *Elgin Hour.* This is an example of how the same producing unit under Herbert Brodkin moved on with a different show title when, as in this case, the sponsor had felt "the price tag was too big." ABC had also felt the price tag was too big, for *U.S. Steel* had stayed on the air during the summer and ABC had had to sustain the alternate show because no sponsor could be found.

This minor series had a major hit with Reginald Rose's topical drama about teenage hoodlums, *Crime in the Streets.* Rose's comments about its preproduction problems seem hard to believe in this day and age!

> It was turned down by the sponsors or advertising agencies of three major network shows for precisely the same reason. It dealt sympathetically with juvenile delinquency at a time when juvenile delinquents were considered to be eminently unpopular.[60]

Rose took issue with a point of view "popular on Madison Avenue" that the function of the entertainment portion of the show "is simply to keep viewers at their sets spellbound . . . so that they will be available to see and hear the ad pitch." Rose argued that simply because a particular show was controversial "it does not necessarily follow that sales of the sponsor's product will drop." As for *Crime in the Streets,* he said he "couldn't for the life of me see what was controversial about it to begin with, and still don't."[61] The Elgin production got high ratings, won enormous praise, and the Elgin Company did not go out of business until quartz and digital watches came along. Even then, its name was good enough to be purchased by a Japanese company.

Creativity — Spectacular and Otherwise

The surge of creativity in live television that had begun in the 1950–51 season lasted through the two seasons from 1953 to 1955. Perhaps 1954–55 was live television's most distinguished season. Prime television and big bucks were *then and now* fully devoted to storytelling. There were successful variety shows, news was getting more attention, and everybody remembers *Howdy Doody*. But 1954–55 saw the "spectaculars" on NBC and CBS rise to great prominence and thankfully demolish forever the sacred cow of regular programming on regular days at regular hours with regular sponsors. It also saw the television writer rise to ever greater prominence as a regular new creative force in our society.

In one sense live drama lacked excitement in the 1953–54 season because most of the "spectaculars" on both networks were content to produce repetitive adaptations of renowned Broadway successes; too much money was involved to take chances. The only changes from the earlier seasons therefore were a more elaborate production in color and more expensive stars. In another sense that season's most "spectacular" successes in many ways were *Kraft Theater*'s relatively inexpensive production of Rod Serling's *Patterns,* and *Studio One*'s series of Reginald Rose dramas.

Jack Gould at the end of that season complained about too much of the "starkly realistic drama," and too many themes dealing with failure:

> There's only one dominant theme on television: Life is hell...
> Television is becoming dour and unentertaining... The Little Person
> in a Little Job in a Little Office who lives in a Little Home with a Little
> Wife and Little Children. He lives in a Little Neighborhood where there
> are Little Minds.[62]

The mass media's programming cycles that flooded the networks with imitations of more successful types had evidently caught up with the hour long dramas. All branches of the entertainment and communications industries have always had trouble with what has been dubbed "follow-the-leader" cycles. Any successful type of book, magazine, play, program, movie or song is quickly followed by hordes of imitations, capitalizing on the success of the original creation. While many of the imitations may be well conceived and executed, as Edmund Rice of *Kraft Theater* commented, "too much of a good thing was no good either." Thus it is seen in a year-end article that *Variety* was concerned with the quantity of morbid, realistic plays, stating that series "are currently at a new high in quantity and a new low in quality." *Variety*'s reporter contended that the older dramatic shows were "still maintaining their standards," pointed to *Lux Video Theater, Climax,* and *Front Row Center* (a summer show that alternated with *U.S. Steel* on CBS) as "clinkers," and listed *Best of Broadway* and the Elgin and Ponds efforts as quality shows that were casualties of the cycle. The article accused the "clinkers" of substituting name stars and name stories for quality. Here is the lineup of the top shows as *Variety* pictured them:

> *Studio One* and *Philco-Goodyear* are in a dead heat for the best in their class, with CBS's Monday Nighter combatting *Philco*'s general superiority in scripts with the slickest producing-directing on television. *Kraft Television Theater* is a strong third, turning out some occasional dull shows but always maintaining a high quality of scripts, production, and integrity. *U.S. Steel* is next but slipping badly of late. *Robert Montgomery Presents* is a tolerable fifth, sometimes turning out top-notch productions but generally falling short of the mark.[63]

The fascinating thing about the first part of the above quotation is that it was as true in 1948–49 as it was in 1954–55, and that it has never happened in broadcasting since and probably never will.

8
The Finale, 1955–58:
Major Players

Sunset in New York

In 1957 television would be available to almost every man,
woman, and child in the United States. By that time there were 496
television stations in the United States and these stations were beaming
programs to approximately 42,000,000 receivers. Television advertising
income had passed the $1.3 billion mark.[1] Television's period of fast
and furious growth was over. It had reached a leveling-off point.

Television production would soon disappear in New York. It
would leave behind television's period of daring and experimentation,
and with it, live television drama. Competition, commercial considera-
tions, ratings, and Hollywood were the keys to television's future. Production costs were up; profits had leveled off as growth had leveled off;
and live dramatic series audience ratings were down. Robert W. Sarnoff
gave one explanation of the situation at a meeting of the NBC affiliates
in 1958:

> For television has become a vast and complex business—far bigger
> than radio ever was, with higher stakes, greater risks and larger areas of
> conflict.
> Because of the variety of conflicting interests and the size of the
> stakes, television has generated fierce and widespread competition,
> perhaps unparalleled in American enterprise. Its cost level is very high,
> calling for large-scale resources. Its total profit—combining all ele-
> ments—is also high, even though spread unevenly across the industry.

Some of the highest risk enterprises, such as networking, have relatively low profit margins...[2]

Interesting it is that this explanation and the young Sarnoff's reign as chief at NBC, accompanied the period of NBC's longest period of turmoil, lowest ratings, and lowest comparable earnings.

Certainly the introduction of magnetic tape recording at this time had a tremendous effect and eventually negated the idea of "live" television production. Several tape recording devices had been demonstrated previously. Bing Crosby enterprises, for example, had made the first demonstration in November 1951.[3] In April of 1956 the Ampex Corporation demonstrated a system that was ready for commercial use in which there was no visible difference between the taped and live picture. The previous tapes were narrow and in order to get all the electrical impulses recorded had to move so fast that a reel the size of a manhole cover was needed. Ampex used a wide tape and several recording heads so a one hour show could be taped on a 14-inch reel. CBS and NBC immediately ordered three each at $75,000 a unit, and the following season they began, without much publicity, taping portions of their shows.[4]

A look at several sample weeks of programming would not seem to indicate that live television was declining. *Playwrights '56* and the fabulous five-days-a-week *Matinee Theater* were new arrivals on NBC in the 1955–56 season and *Armstrong Circle Theater* expanded to a full hour. Max Liebman presented only a few "spectaculars," but *Hallmark Hall of Fame* was now a 90-minute show once a month, *Producer's Showcase* was in its second season, and CBS introduced its first once-a-month, 90-minute "spectacular," *Ford Star Jubilee.* It was followed by one of CBS's most famous and successful undertakings — *Playhouse 90.*

On the other hand the *Lux Video Theater* dispensed with live drama in December of 1956, and at the end of that season, *Alcoa-Goodyear, Kaiser Aluminum, Robert Montgomery Presents,* and *Producer's Showcase* were eliminated from NBC. The end was in sight. Industry personnel were predicting the two-hour drama as a regular series was just around the corner. However, Ford bowed out of its commitment to *Ford Star Jubilee* at season's end and the industry re-evaluated its rush into live 90-minute programming. Very few of the "spectaculars" had cracked the lists of the ten most popular shows, and, perhaps, the fabulously successful *Peter Pan* had led some producers to expect more than they could get. *Kraft, Philco Playhouse* (now also *Alcoa*), *Studio One* and several live variety shows maintained steady ratings and satisfied the sponsors. In fact, 1956 was a great year for Ed Sullivan. He was in high gear, introducing Elvis Presley (from the waist up) to immortality that year.

Live television drama had been the pacesetter in terms of quality for the first ten years of television. The format had withstood the flood of situation comedies, mysteries, feature films, quiz and variety shows. Yet in the next two short years the filmed Western would do what all the other mediocre forms of entertainment had failed to do.

Some of the external reasons for live television's demise have been mentioned but it is also true there was a goodly amount of internal strangulation. At the time of the 1956–57 season either the quality of the drama had fallen off or the reviewers were getting harder to please. In an industry that tends to flamboyance, the reviewers had fewer kind things to say about the series dramas than ever before. For example, a series of eight reviews in the *New York Times* gave eight *Kraft Television Theater* productions bad or barely mediocre reviews. The productions, all in 1955, were:

Woman for Tony, June 2
Someone to Hang, June 9
Truckers Welcome, October 13
I, Mrs. Bibb, October 20
Ticket and Tempest, November 10
Summers End, November 17
Once a Genius, December 1
A Nugget from the Sunrise, December 15

It was true that the exodus of the television writer to the lucrative field of motion pictures was a factor but there was no evidence of the creative climate that had fostered writers such as Rose, Chayefsky, Mosel and Serling. *Playhouse 90* was brilliant during these final seasons and maybe the rest of them were just plain worn out. For example, the use of topical drama increased in the attempt to find good script material. *Armstrong Circle Theater* in 1955 devoted itself to finding drama in the current scene; a typical Armstrong title was "S.O.S. from the Andrea Doria." In 1956–57 Kraft did Mickey Mantle's life story, and the Hungarian revolt stimulated scripts on *Studio One, Armstrong,* and the *Hall of Fame*'s revival of Sherwood's "There Shall Be No Night."

High Noon in Hollywood

In contrast to the bright, if not big, successes of films on television, live drama television was unexciting. In 1955–56 *Playhouse 90* and *Matinee Theater* were still to come, but the success of CBS's *Gunsmoke* and ABC's *Wyatt Earp* had everyone in Hollywood looking for an adult Western to do. As Hal Humphrey said in *The Los Angeles Mirror*, "It was more frantic than the old Oklahoma land rush of 1889," and "by the following season adult Westerns had multiplied like jackrabbits."⁵

The towering success of the Western series *Gunsmoke* provided the stimulus for the domination of film on prime time television. As usual in the mass media, the maiden creative effort had more quality than its imitators. And in this case it is fitting that the original idea came from the broadcasting industry, a marvelous old radio show called *Gunsmoke* that started in 1952 and ran until 1961. This radio version of *Gunsmoke* was acclaimed critically right from the start but CBS could not get it sponsored until it had been on the air for a year. Drama had had a long and successful tradition when radio was the magic medium and a number of radio dramas moved directly over to live television, including *Lux Video Theater* and *Armstrong Circle Theater*. This first radio drama to move to film on television was created in 1952 by a CBS radio producer named Norman Macdonnell, who, with writer John Meston, is given credit by Hal Humphrey in the *Los Angeles Mirror* for fighting valiantly to retain on television the simple plots and adult flavor they had created on radio.⁶

Huber Ellinsworth in a delightful essay in a media textbook compared the radio and television versions:

> Certainly the best adult Western, and perhaps the most artistically superior radio series ever produced, was *Gunsmoke*. Marshal Dillon (William Conrad) stayed alive by shooting first and talking later. And when he rode into Dodge after days on the trail and growled, "Where's Kitty?", listeners knew why he was asking. Kitty (Georgia Ellis) ran a tough saloon, the Long Branch, with rooms upstairs definitely not operated by Sheraton. Life was hard and violent and people died of wounds, starvation, freezing, and childbirth, sometimes aided by hard-drinking Doc Adams. A later TV version of this program portrayed Dillon as a gun-toting frontier psychiatrist who brought order and mental health to the snow-capped mountain region of central Kansas. The TV Dillon hung out at the Long Branch YMCA, which inexplicably served liquor but was kept respectable by housemother Miss Kitty.⁷

Films made for television had been increasing slowly over the years and mostly were the "here today and gone tomorrow" sitcoms. All of a sudden film was a glut as the networks carried an impressive 1,151 hours of film, an increase of 286 hours in 1955–56.[8] The major portion of the increase was the Westerns. The television screen had never lacked for Western drama in the form of old feature films. But whereas in prime evening time in 1954 there was only one Western series especially made for television, *The Lone Ranger;* in 1958–59 there were 23! In six months in 1956 eleven new Western series were started on the three networks.[9]

"Trend?" said one NBC Los Angeles head. "It's an avalanche." The "follow the leader" cycle of all mass media was carried to one of its most notable extremes ever.

The avalanche (or stampede) to Western films was the prime responsibility of the American Broadcasting Company. ABC had constantly failed in its efforts to compete on the same level with the "big" networks. It has been shown how CBS "stole" *Studio One* from ABC. Finally in 1954 ABC had the first big success that was not lured away by the bigger networks—the late afternoon Walt Disney show on film. Thereupon, ABC made another challenge that season to CBS-NBC leadership. Clearance for live schedules had always been a great problem to ABC, and film was an obvious answer. In the fall of 1955, ABC put Wyatt Earp and Cheyenne on the air, they were moderately successful, and the die was cast.

We indicated that the starting gun for the great rush was fired by *Gunsmoke* on CBS and it was an instantaneous and much-heralded success. It was quickly followed by *Frontier* and *Fury* in 1955–56, *Jim Bowie, Wells Fargo, Broken Arrow* and *Zane Grey Theater* in 1956–57 and *Have Gun Will Travel, Trackdown, Maverick, Sugarfoot, Tombstone, Colt '45, Restless Gun, Wagon Train, The Californians,* and *Union Pacific* in 1957–58. Nine of these were ABC shows as compared with four each for the other networks. Live television drama by no means bore the full brunt of the onslaught. The comedians who had been having such success on television began to pass out of the picture. Jackie Gleason, Sid Caesar and Imogene Coca, and George Gobel were among the fatalities. CBS placed *Gunsmoke* opposite George Gobel, and his Saturday evening show was cancelled. The sponsors were impressed with ABC's ratings. In 1953 ABC nighttime programs had led the networks in only two half-hours. In the fall of 1956 ABC led in ten nighttime half-hours, in comparison with NBC's nine half-hours and CBS's 23 half-hours.[10] The Madison Avenue merchants were winning the battle for control of broadcasting. The producers and creators would become their servants and the ad agencies' modes of operation would bear little relationship to the tradition of creative production established by the ad agency pioneer, J. Walter Thompson.

Feature Films, Front and Center

If it was *Gunsmoke* that fired the gun, then it was the Hollywood feature film that put the nails in New York television's coffin. An examination of the television schedules of 1957–58 reveals the results of the many multimillion dollar motion picture deals that had been announced in 1955 and 1956. Live drama faced the dual threat of old and new films. The economic boycott of television by the filmmakers was past history. Hollywood had been holding back on its great reservoir of entertainment, and when it let go there was a deluge of proven entertainment. Part of the reason for holding back was what was known as the feature film bottleneck of 1948. That date marked the time after which additional payments must be made to certain personnel associated with a picture if it was re-run on television. Also the last of the pre-1948 films were being released. The scope of those operations was indicated by one sale of 750 Paramount pictures to the Music Corporation of America for $50 million. Some of the fine old films discovered on television for the first time that season were: *Mutiny on the Bounty, David Copperfield, The Yearling*, several Greta Garbo films, *The Foxes of Harrow, Les Misérables, The Ox-Bow Incident, Champion, Notorious, Hamlet*, and *Cry, the Beloved Country*.

The live network dramas now faced a stiffer film competition than ever before. One aspect of this situation was that Hollywood, through companies such as National Telefilms, was selling pictures to independent stations in the major markets such as New York and Los Angeles. Thus a proven and highly publicized feature film was competing with a one hour drama of unknown quality. The viewer was no longer passing up the independent station. For example, WOR, the DuMont station in New York, had a huge rating increase as a result of its *Million Dollar Movie* series, and local stations in cities all across the country were selling advertising on a scale that began to worry the national sponsors.[11]

The Erosion of Network Leadership

Symptomatic of live television's troubles was the resignation in 1956 of Pat Weaver from NBC because of "policy differences." During Weaver's tenure, CBS overtook NBC in nighttime program ratings and stayed ahead. Under the new Robert Kintner–Robert Lewine programming regime, "spectaculars" became "specials" on NBC, and live drama was dropped in order to compete with the Westerns.[12] In April of 1957 Pat Weaver's announcement of his temporary re-entrance into broadcasting was accompanied by thrusts at the networks, alleging they were not able to do their jobs for the public "because of inter-network warfare based on program ratings and high costs...." He accused them of mediocre programming aimed at "moppets, morons, and idiots, who will look at anything."[13] Robert Austin Smith in an article in *Fortune* magazine, "Television, the Light That Failed," looked back over the "increasing mediocrity" in television and cited "a score of seemingly unrelated happenings" that were causes: "The exodus of creative talent from television; the erosion of the network leadership in the East; and the coming of age of the film packagers." But more than anything else he flattered Weaver by citing his departure from the chairmanship of NBC as "the precipitating incident." He stated Weaver was looked upon by many "as a sort of personification of television's potential scope, dynamism and audacity," and accused NBC of "playing it safe and small."[14]

The charge of "erosion of network leadership" in New York was made repeatedly in the press from 1955 on. It was true that the *Lux Video, Hall of Fame, Climax, Playhouse 90,* and eventually the *Studio One* series would emanate from Hollywood. However, most producers and executives interviewed failed to see this as a significant aspect of live television drama's decline. Robert Sarnoff, in an open letter to newspaper editors, answered the charges that the whole television industry was shifting to the West Coast:

> The NBC headquarters is in New York, and will remain here. Our New York studios are being used to capacity. Our yardstick for deciding on East or West Coast origination for any particular program is availability of talent and production facilities. Right now we have a good balance between the two coasts and I expect it will remain in reasonable balance.[15]

That part of the programming upheaval that received the most publicity was the audience ratings services. Florence Britton, in the last edition of *Best Television Plays,* sorrowfully complained about the low ratings of the series dramas as the basic cause of the decline:

> Nineteen fifty-six–fifty-seven was not a vintage year in television. Perhaps this is understandable in a medium that is still trying to find a compromise among creativity, audience appeal, and omnipresent fact that it is in business primarily due to the modern Medici, the advertiser.[16]

David Suskind, a Harvard graduate who became an agent and then a producer for Talent Associates, rose to great prominence in these years through his vigorous defense of live drama when everyone had written it off. He had worked on the *Philco* show, the *Kaiser Aluminum Hour,* the *DuPont Show of the Month,* and others. When interviewed in *Broadcasting-Telecasting* in 1957 he said:

> The only exciting TV I've ever seen has been live. I am utterly unable to remember any distinguished filmed TV. All the filmed TV I've seen has been distinguished by a kind of uniform mediocrity and by an economy of shooting and production which make it pretty lacklustre as entertainment. On the other hand, *Peter Pan, Cinderella, Marty, The Rainmaker, Requiem for a Heavyweight, The Helen Keller Story, A Night to Remember*—the list of live distinguished accomplishments in TV—is extremely long.
>
> I also have the feeling that there is a different philosophy governing the doing of live shows. Filmed shows are being made, for the most part, by "get-rich-quick" people who regard television not as an art form or an area for creative expression, but as an opportunity (like a gold mine or an oil well) to accomplish endless residuals, to be able to live unto the fourth generation on the income from fast and cheap production. I find this shocking and I loathe it . . .
>
> The real film giants are not the men making TV film. The TV films of today are made by has-beens and never-weres in the film business— by people hell bent for capital gains deals. When you see a film that says "George Stevens directed and produced"—you can bet your money it's going to be a good show. These people are above and beyond television films now and the people who are doing TV films are not equipped by God or talent to do the job. What you're getting are lacklustre extensions of their feeble talents.[17]

In an address in Ithaca, New York, in 1958, Robert Lewine, vice president in charge of programming at NBC, answered some of the charges being made about film:

There is the complaint that the television industry is switching increasingly from live shows to film, and accordingly, from the invigorating intellectual climate of New York to the arid wastes of Hollywood. Well, it just isn't so. It is true that over the years, the use of film has increased. I can't see anything wrong with that.

Live television has an irreplaceable quality of its own. By the same token, film gives the storyteller a range, flexibility and variety of visual power that cannot be achieved in any other way. There are certain stories — any outdoor story is an obvious example — that are more effective on film. But I do not see any danger that film will crowd live TV off the home screen. . . [18]

Playhouse 90 and Hubbell Robinson, Jr.

It was not all over yet and Sarnoff's defense of live television seemed reasonable at that time. Many new provocative and impressive things continued to happen on live television and most were live television drama — even if they were out of the mainstream. The most extraordinary of these was *Playhouse 90*. It was only mid-course in live television's decline, and CBS, with Martin Manulis as the producer, undertook one of television's most ambitious undertakings, *Playhouse 90*. They sought to present a 90-minute drama every week using Pat Weaver's magazine concept to finance it. CBS President Frank Stanton reasoned: "One trouble with the 'specials' is that people haven't known where they are." [19]

Hubbell Robinson, Jr. was a distinguished executive at CBS in the creative tradition of NBC's Pat Weaver. When interviewed he took full credit for creating *Playhouse 90:*

> I thought it up. We had done a series, *Best of Broadway*, that was one hour, and we couldn't adapt Broadway plays successfully to the one hour format.
>
> I thought that 90 minutes would open us up to more material. I sent a two page memo recommending it to Paley [CBS Chairman]. We had a hell of a time getting it started. They said we couldn't do it. They said we could never sell it. We took 15 months preparing it. [20]

Hubbell Robinson had played a major role in creating shows for CBS. He stated "I was very close to *Playhouse 90* all throughout. I found the first property — the show we opened with." [21] This show was Rod Serling's adaptation of a Pat Frank novel, *Forbidden Area*. Most of the reviewers felt it was not "a very auspicious debut,"[22] but they returned the following week with a smash hit, *Requiem for a Heavyweight,* also by Rod Serling.

Requiem for a Heavyweight won five of the major prizes in the Emmy awards, the first Peabody Award for script writing, and the Sylvania award as the best play of the year — all of the major honors in broadcasting.[23] Rod Serling and most of the reviewers felt that Jack Palance gave "a performance of indescribable poignancy" in the role of an inarticulate, has-been prize fighter who is told by his physician that he cannot continue fighting. His avaricious manager then tries to use him as a wrestling clown to pay his own gambling debts. However, his compassionate trainer and a social worker arrange for him to go home, and it ends with a vision of his finding another life for himself.[24]

Playhouse 90 in a live and then a taped version was the quality dramatic feature of network broadcasting for the next three seasons and most television audiences remember it better than shows such as *Philco* and *Kraft* because it lasted so long into broadcasting's film era. One CBS public relations vice president, Leonard Spinrad, pointed to *Playhouse 90* and stated that many of the live shows that passed away "simply were not comparable in terms of quality." He concluded, "We're better off without so many; we had *Studio One,* now we have *Playhouse 90.*"[25] Lester Bernstein, NBC vice president, agreed that *Playhouse 90* on CBS was an excellent show: "We had too many, and now it's an only outlet."[26] This certainly was a factor in *Playhouse 90*'s success in succeeding years. For example, in November of 1957 Fred Coe resigned from NBC on the grounds he was not being given anything to do. Hubbell Robinson immediately signed him up for CBS to produce part of the *Playhouse 90* series with Herbert Brodkin and John Houseman. Martin Manulis had relinquished his producing role at the end of the 1957–58 season to do films for 20th Century–Fox.[27]

In just one month, March of 1957, *Playhouse 90* started on March 7 with Gilbert Roland, Hugh O'Brien, Ann Bancroft and Ray Collins in *Invitation to a Gunfighter.* This was followed on March 14 with Jack Palance, Viveca Lindfors, Peter Lorre and Keenan Wynn in *The Last Tycoon.* Then they came up with an unusual cast and a hit performance of *Hostess with the Mostest* with Perle Mesta, Shirley Booth and Hedda Hopper on March 21. There was no letdown as they concluded the month on the 28th with Art Carney, Jeanette MacDonald and Jackie Cooper in *Charley's Aunt.*

Hubbell Robinson felt that the first two years of *Playhouse 90* were the very best television he had seen and "Martin Manulis agrees with me." He grumbled a little that "In the third year we had some good shows with Brodkin and Coe but there were some bad ones." And then he somewhat sadly reminisced:

> The fourth year was *Playhouse*'s worst year. *No* one was sitting on it, guiding it, working for quality. The producers were doing the things they always wanted to do. Also there was a tremendous rash of specials that year and it did not stand out as much as it had in the past. Also actors were getting more money for specials and we couldn't afford them on that budget.[28]

Albert McCleery commented that its producers became competitive, started "bidding against one another and it collapsed."[29]

Hubbell Robinson, Jr. was the other "missing" executive that journalists point to when they bewail the fate of television over the next ten years. He stated, "I left CBS because I was given the opportunity to set up my own company and own my own programs." He was very definite that he liked "working directly with Paley and it was a happy relationship." His break with CBS did not parallel the explosive outbursts about the Sarnoffs and Weaver. But he was glum in thinking about it: "I created all those shows and all I got was a salary and a pension and I might not live long enough to collect the pension."[30]

Albert McCleery indicated to this writer that the decline of live television was rather simple: "It was the victim of the ratings systems as they reflect cost per thousand." So as we move to look at McCleery's monumental achievement in *Matinee Theater* it is appropriate to note that he felt "*Playhouse 90* killed live drama by making it so expensive," claiming "Martin Manulis' prices were astronomical, an average of $175,000 per show." "Of course," McCleery said, "you can't do *Marty* on film anyway—no scope, no glamour—just *beauty*."[31]

Matinee Theater, the "Most Formidable" Undertaking

If *Playhouse 90* was the most extraordinary show in live television's last years, then *Matinee Theater* was the most formidable. Jane Murray, the talented casting director for that series and many more, shared her 50 page outline of its accomplishments. She began it:

12 noon in Hollywood and 3 p.m. in New York.
Opening drum roll and NBC peacock film.
JOHN CONTE voice over: "The following program is brought to you in
    living color by NBC."
MATINEE theme music up synchronized with MATINEE kaleidoscope
    pattern.
MATINEE logos. CONTE voice over: "MATINEE THEATER"...
    (flip card)
"devised and produced for NBC by ALBERT McCLEERY"...
    (flip card)
"presents" ... title of show, author and adapter ... audio credit to
    stars of show.
Slowly dissolve into teaser.
End of teaser, kaleidoscope pattern, CONTE host set.
CONTE: "Hello, everyone. Welcome once again to NBC MATINEE
    THEATER for another hour-long presentation brought to you live
    and in living color. I am your host, John Conte."[32]

This same opening with very slight variations greeted viewers five
days a week from October 31, 1955, until June 27, 1958, through a total
of 666 shows. This was an enormous accomplishment in the history of
drama, of all story-telling through the ages. NBC's *Matinee Theater*
amassed that staggering total of 666 hour-long dramatic shows live, in
color, from Hollywood, in the short space of 36 months! They did
classics, original drama, Broadway, and stories on current events, with
many good reviews from the most sophisticated critics and with a large
audience and a profit for the network. McCleery described how the idea
developed:

> I have about ten memos on show ideas that I reissue annually. One
> of these memos dealt with an idea for a daily midnight mysteries. I had
> been sending out numerous memos on it. On the 15th of June 1955,
> Pat Weaver sent for me and said: "Do you think you can do an hour
> show every day at three p.m.?" I said "yes." Then later in New York,
> Pat Weaver dictated a thirty page memo of what he wanted *Matinee
> Theater* to be. It was a beautiful thing. We did not fully understand
> it but it called for the birth of a great new theater, a springboard for
> the great actors, directors, and playwrights of the future.[33]

Laurels are again due to Pat Weaver. Parts of this memo are included in an Appendix to the present work (see pages 129–145). He
mentions in it that soap operas "began to rear their ugly heads" and
transfer from radio to television. This series was to be different, to have
each performance as complete in itself in order to set it apart.

There are again special laurels for Albert McCleery. He joked that "General Sarnoff used to introduce me as the only man on the staff who's making more money than him." The evidence and the comments of his staff indicate he worked hard for it. Everyone connected with *Matinee Theater* came off as "inspired by McCleery's leadership." There was a unique "kinship with the show" among everyone, the writers, directors, actors and production personnel. Jane Murray explained, "The selection of the man was crucial — an organizational genius and a genius in his production techniques." She was excited about what they had accomplished and said ten years later that actors have been coming into her office ever since and saying, "Oh, remember, that *Matinee Theater* show we did."[34]

Of course, most actors found live television to be more rewarding than film. In live television, as Jane Murray said, actors found themselves closer to the final result. The contributions were their own in contrast to film or video tape, which "can be recut and scored." These media "deemphasize the faults of actors and they know it." So Hollywood actors, the famous and successful included, came in droves with special eagerness to be a part of *Matinee Theater*. It was such an "unusual experiment" and McCleery gave it a special "cohesive spirit." "I look back and am glad to have been a part of it," said Jane Murray; "there was something *alive* about everything he [McCleery] did. The big thing was the excitement. Can you imagine the difficulties — five live dramas a week, every week. We did it — a sort of camaraderie infused by McCleery overcame the difficulties." This was an interesting interview. This lady was inspired by a sense of personal accomplishment by having been a part of *Matinee Theater*.[35]

No doubt *Matinee Theater* had its share of "potboilers," but overall it received good critical notices. McCleery explained:

> I've been very lucky in this way. I have worked on a quantity basis and I have outstanding shows that people point to. If I suspected ahead that I was about to do something good then I could go to bat for it. I could publicize it. The bad ones I could hide. Someone like Coe has to go to bat every time, so I have the better batting average on reviews.[36]

No doubt, also, that McCleery's organizational genius was a factor in their success. He assembled a group of talented personnel and devised new and simplified working methods to keep the operation efficient. He focused on his old "cameo" style of production and rather than five competing producers for the five weekly shows, he used three: a script producer, a casting producer, and a technical producer.

There are many interesting stories to come out of the 666 shows; for example, a show was never cancelled for internal reasons. In one instance an actor called up seriously ill the morning of the performance. The director, Dennis Patrick, called McCleery and suggested cancellation. "Dennis, do you know the lines?" He was not sure, but McCleery suggested he "try it on the first dress rehearsal." The idea had not occurred to Patrick but in the best tradition of the theater, the show went on — "without a hitch."

Also, in the best tradition of the theater, the show eventually closed. In its third year *Matinee Theater* started to lose money and was replaced by two Proctor and Gamble soap operas. A novel effort was made to save the show by appealing for public financial support — "a dollar a year per viewer." Mrs. Ruth Conte, wife of John Conte, the host of the series, was the initiator of this plea. Executives at NBC expressed distress at the efforts, stating they would only end in embarrassment for the network. They said they invested $12 million in the show and that it was showing a $3 million net loss.[37] McCleery commented:

> Conte thought he could force NBC into retaining it. This is ridiculous. Three hundred twenty-five thousand did come in voluntarily and not one donation more than five dollars. It could have been millions if NBC had publicly asked for it. This was a stillborn version of pay TV. If you don't believe it was popular, ask my wife. There was also an enormous male audience — men who worked at night. And the captive type audiences, such as hospitals. One Superintendent of Nursing wrote in and let them know her patients demanded not to be disturbed with needles and meals during *Matinee Theater*. We did about 200 classics and schools came to a dead halt as the kids met in the auditorium and watched it.[38]

9
The Finale, 1955–58:
Supporting Cast

The Alcoa-Goodyear Playhouse

Although one of *Philco-Goodyear Playhouse*'s sponsors returned in 1955, the Sunday night drama on NBC was produced by an entirely new organization. Thus the Philco Corporation was not associated with the declining years of live television drama. The new producing organization was Showcase Productions and Herbert Brodkin of the ABC Motorola and Elgin hours was hired as producer. He deprecated any attempts to link the show with its predecessor: "It's a new show."[1] It produced several interesting originals by Reginald Rose, and its more successful writers, such as John Gay, moved quickly to Hollywood.

This series had only a moderate success and lasted only two seasons. It arrived at the end of live television drama's "golden years" and passed quickly out of the picture with the older series. Most writers and the NBC Press Department misleadingly pictured it as simply a continuation of the *Philco-Goodyear* show in its declining years. No, the honored live dramatic series ended quickly and quietly, a class act to the very end.

Kraft Television Theater, the Lone Survivor

The J. Walter Thompson Agency had its first indication in 1955 that live television drama was in its last big year. For the first time in eight years the *Kraft Television Theater* found its audience ratings below the CBS competition, *I've Got a Secret* and *Masquerade Party*.[2] *Kraft* also got an indication of how the demand for scripts had grown steadily in the past few years. After a suggestion by Ed Rice, *Kraft* offered $50,000 to the author of the best original play of their season. A number of other organizations were by that time giving cash awards to television scripts. Four of the more important ones, the Fund for the Republic, the Robert E. Sherwood Award, the B'nai B'rith Award, and the Christopher Award, had propaganda motivations.[3]

The announced purpose of the *Kraft* award was "to give proper recognition to distinguished achievement in the field of dramatic television writing."[4] A number of writers complained in letters to the editor that they would like it better if *Kraft* raised the price for every script instead of overpaying for one. Edmund Rice stated that "it was very difficult" to tell whether the award attracted new writers to *Kraft* or gained them any scripts, but "I believe it did get us some very good scripts that we would not otherwise have gotten; but it is impossible to tell." He felt there was a serious shortage of "good scripts" at that time, but then "there always was and always will be a shortage of 'good' art in any creative endeavor."[5] The winning play, *Snapfinger Creek*, by William Noble, was chosen by Helen Hayes, Maxwell Anderson and Walter Kerr. Script editor Florence Britton said of it: "In my opinion, *Snapfinger Creek* is pure television; it could not possibly be realized in any other medium."[6] In many ways the play does seem typical of live television scripts. It has a minimum of plot incident and is centered on an intimate revelation of the family life of Southern farm folk. It was based on a Georgia legend that if you can snap your fingers three times while running "lickety-split" over the short Snapfinger Creek bridge, any wish will come true. Farming cotton has left the family portrayed as poor but not without pride and abiding love for each other. When the daughter falls in love with a young man whom she feels is beyond her reach, her family rallies to her side to make her dream possible.[7]

Kraft achieved a major event in the history of live television drama that season with its production of an adaptation of the Walter Lord book, *A Night to Remember*. This re-enactment of the last hours of the *Titanic* was chosen by Rice as the *Kraft* play that "stands out so much over all the others."[8] It received great critical acclaim and the largest number of complimentary letters in the history of the dramatic series.

Its kinescope was replayed on May 2 to celebrate the start of *Kraft*'s tenth year on NBC. It had a cast of 107 and used 31 different sets. John Crosby in the *Herald Tribune* described it as "far and away the most complex production in television's history":

> The greatest single thing about *Kraft*'s marvelous production..., was simply that it was done at all on live television... I bring up all of this technical detail because it contributed enormously to the show's impact.[9]

And Jack Gould wrote:

> The production was an extraordinary demonstration of staging technique that imparted a magnificent sense of physical dimension to the home screen... The emotional tension and terrifying suspense were effectively introduced and for the most part well sustained.[10]

Variety, too, was delighted:

> A brilliant feat from any angle. If any show rated the spectacular tag, this was it.[11]

Edmund Rice remarked about the replay of the kinescope film that they wouldn't have dared to attempt it over again live, as they had *Patterns* the season before. He told how the production came about:

> The book was written by a man at J. Walter Thompson—a copy writer. We thought the book was great. We had no idea how we would do it—it seemed impossible. The manner of presenting it that struck us as we often sat around talking about it was to use the form of a court investigation—after the fact. This enabled us to logically select incidents we would use. The book had hundreds and hundreds of tiny incidents and as we got more and more wrapped up in it, it was a job selecting what incidents to include.
> I think George Roy Hill [the director] is the only one who could have done it, and I doubt if he could do it again. Everything was perfect. Hundreds of cues and not a single one missed.
> It was a major production job and extremely expensive. We were way over our budget. It just had to be a success. We took a great chance; so were so far over [the budget] that we could not get a check from *Kraft* until after the performance when they saw if it was worth it.[12]

When asked what *Kraft* productions stood out in his memory, Rice also mentioned two other plays produced that season. The plays were *Death Is a Spanish Dancer* and *No Riders* by Wendall Mayes and by an unusual coincidence they were the two *Kraft* plays cited by Florence

Britton in the appendix to her book, *Best Television Plays, 1957,* as "television plays worthy of note."[13] Rice told how *Death Is a Spanish Dancer* was a play that came to them unsolicited:

> But it was too poetical. We couldn't do it but I got hold of the writer to get something else from him. So he wrote other plays for us. It was Wendall Mayes. He was getting good critical notices and attention, so we decided we would take a chance on the first script he had submitted *[Death Is a Spanish Dancer].*
>
> I was really unhappy with the production it received. I think that it is the most beautiful play we ever did.
>
> Wendall Mayes is now in Hollywood. They [the television playwrights] left us fast. He's doing the screen play for *Anatomy of a Murder.*[14]

The play was inspired by Mexican legend that "death may take the attractive form of a Spanish dancer." Kim Stanley portrayed the girl of the legend, who was irresistibly drawn to a Spanish dancer she sees in a night club. She is in delicate health, and her family seeks to protect her. They have the club closed, but she leaves home and finds her fatal love again.[15] It seems strange that Rice was unhappy with the production. Perhaps it was the script or actress Stanley, but it was delightful for the viewer.

By 1957–58, *Kraft Television Theater* was the lone survivor of the live weekly series in New York. In April of 1958 J. Walter Thompson handed over the production reins to Talent Associates, and for several weeks it looked as if *Kraft* was headed for new glories. Under producer Robert T. Herridge, a bill of one-act plays by Tennessee Williams and a two-part adaptation of *All the King's Men* received excellent reviews.[16] But the word was let out in early May that *Kraft* would not be back in 1958–59. Part of the reason expressed had to do with the purchase of Kraft Foods Corporation by National Dairy Products Corporation. Although the newspapers claimed other divisions of National Dairy Products wanted to use that time for setting up their own shows, undoubtedly the fact that *Kraft* did not enjoy as high ratings as it once had was the major reason.[17]

In June 1958, the show became *Kraft Mystery Theater* and in October, after 11 years and five months, *Kraft Theater* closed its doors with its 650th drama, *Presumption of Innocence.* It was replaced by two half-hour shows, *Milton Berle* and *Bat Masterson.*[18] Since the first *Kraft* show, *Double Door* on May 7, 1947, the series had been off the air only twice—in June of 1948 and 1952 when it was pre-empted by presidential conventions. The Kraft Foods Corporation also deserved much credit. *Kraft* producer Maury Holland said in 1957:

> Our sponsor is more understanding than others, allows us to make a certain number of mistakes... We're judged on over-all performance rather than one show. As sponsors go this is unique.[19]

Fred Coe and Playwrights '56

Fred Coe was not associated with *Producer's Showcase* that season. He opened a new series, *Playwrights '56,* that alternated with the *Armstrong Circle Theater.* In it Coe continued the work he had been doing with playwrights on the *Philco Playhouse.* His staff for the new series were his *Philco Playhouse* associates, including directors Arthur Penn and Vincent Donahue. In Coe's past work he had shown his recognition of the importance of the writer as a basic ingredient to success. In this series the NBC files credit him as having "held out for the inclusion of 'playwright' in the title," an indication of his continuing concentration on the writer.[20]

When Albert McCleery was asked about "commerical intrusion" and "censorship" of television drama he mentioned *Playwrights '56:*

> They've [the sponsors] got their rights and they exercise them. If you let an artist go undisciplined there is bound to be an asceticism set in. For example, with *Playwrights '56* Coe had a contract with Pontiac that gave him complete freedom. But an artist given his head will not consider, for example, the atmosphere in which the commercial will succeed. That is, we must create an attitude that will be favorable to the commercial. When that lipstick was my sponsor I couldn't do a bloody scene right before the commercial on a color show. I did a show about a gangster who had a girl friend who was dying of TB. This girl coughed all through the show and the cigarette sponsor complained. I had just completely forgotten the tie-up with cigarettes. I felt the sponsor was right.[21]

When asked if his contract on *Playwrights '56* gave him carte blanche, Coe replied:

> That's a silly thing to say. It's much more complicated than that. Nobody has carte blanche in television; that's not the way it is done. After you reach a certain stage they [the sponsors] have faith in you

and respect you. They will stand by you on what you think is right.[22]

Evidently Coe did have a good bit of freedom of operation with *Playwrights '56*. It was of the same type of freedom that Rice described when speaking of *Kraft Theater:*

> From a personal point of view we never had any trouble. You have to take a firm stand. We had the respect of our client. They respected our ability and our taste. They had to believe we had these if we were going to succeed in the long run with any kind of working relationship.[23]

At the end of the season Pontiac announced it had asked to be relieved of the sponsorship of *Playwrights '56* and was switching its budget to *Wide Wide World*. When asked what was the basis of Pontiac's decision to switch its advertising budget, Coe replied:

> *Playwrights '56* was an hour show every other week alternating with *Armstrong Circle Theater*. Each show had a very specific problem; each had different advertising aims and the two shows were very opposite in their aims. Pontiac wanted a very distinct sales message to a large audience. *Armstrong Circle* had in mind sponsor identification with a special type of show. The two shows did not go together. For Pontiac ratings were too low and it withdrew.[24]

In its one season *Playwrights '56* produced a number of distinctive new dramas though most were not as critically successful as the *Philco* dramas had been. *The Waiting Place* by Tad Mosel in December was described by the author as his best play. Kim Stanley played the central character, a 14-year-old girl. "I wanted it to be a play about people who wait." For the young girl the waiting place is a ravine where she waits for things to happen and acts out the things she imagines should happen. For her father it is the mill; for her grandmother it is the wheelchair; and for her future stepmother it is the kitchen. The conflict evolves around the overpossessiveness of the young girl for her widowed father and his desire to remarry.[25] *Variety* wrote about Coe's casting:

> For about the first ten minutes . . . it looked as if Producer Fred Coe had flipped his lid. Imagine casting Kim Stanley as a 14-year-old. But after those first few minutes they could have called him Canny Coe, for Miss Stanley was not only completely believable in the part, but delivered one of the stunning virtuoso performances of this or any other season.[26]

Producer's Showcase, Hallmark Hall of Fame, Ford Star Jubilee

After a production of a musical version of *Our Town* with Frank Sinatra, Eva Marie Saint, and Paul Newman, Fred Coe left *Producer's Showcase* to do the new *Playwrights '56* series. The Sinatra, Saint and Newman production was described by reviewers as "90 minutes of magnificent entertainment." It was a risky gamble adding *music* to an established modern classic "but it lost none of its charm."[27]

Donald Davis and his wife Dorothy Mathews became the new producers for *Producer's Showcase*. Some productions of interest that season were *Cyrano de Bergerac* with Jose Ferrar and Claire Bloom, *Caesar and Cleopatra* with Sir Cedric Hardwicke and Claire Bloom, and *The Barretts of Wimpole Street* with Anthony Quayle and Katherine Cornell. *Peter Pan* was repeated on January 9, 1956, to an estimated 55 million viewers.[28] Indicative of the importance of Fred Coe to the original production was the insistence of Mary Martin and her husband that Coe be the producer of the repeat performance. To win their point, a "we love Coe" advertisement was printed in the *New York Times* at their expense. At that point Jerome Robbins, who had staged the show originally, threatened to walk out on the repeat production. NBC mollified everyone by issuing a denial that Coe would produce and gave him an unofficial "advisory" status.[29] At the end of that season *Producer's Showcase* was given an Emmy and a Peabody Award for dramatic entertainment.[30]

NBC's second 90-minute dramatic series, *Hall of Fame*, changed its facade that season. For this one season it was called *Maurice Evans Presents the Hallmark Hall of Fame*. Maurice Evans was host for their eight monthly productions, starred in two productions, and was listed as producer of the series. Jack Rayel was NBC executive producer, George Schaefer directed, and Mildred Freed Albert was associate producer.[31] The scuttlebutt was that Maurice Evans was just the host and a performer and that the creative work was done by Jack Rayel. The two shows that Evans starred in were Shaw's *The Devil's Disciple* and Shakespeare's *Taming of the Shrew*. *Cradle Song* in May with Judith Anderson, Anthony Franciosa, and Siobhan McKenna received unusually flowery notices: "To have missed *The Cradle Song* yesterday afternoon was to have missed one of the most beautiful and deeply stirring programs that television has ever offered."[32]

CBS played broadcasting's "follow-the-leader" and came up with its own ten different 90-minute color "spectaculars." Jack Gould stated simply: "The historic pattern of broadcasting is now all but junked."[33] The premiere production in the *Ford Star Jubilee* was *The Caine Mutiny Court Martial.* It was the most successful of the group. Others such as *High Tor,* a filmed musical version with Bing Crosby, and *Blithe Spirit* with Noel Coward received mixed reviews and for the sponsor, disappointing audience ratings.[34] In *The Caine Mutiny Court Martial* Lloyd Nolan recreated his honored interpretation of Captain Queeg and "it gained magnificence on television." It was described in the *Times* as "ninety minutes of brilliant television theater,"[35] and "one of the most arresting and rewarding dramas of the season."[36]

From the very beginning of this series the newspapers and magazines were full of articles on one wrangle after another between the Ford Motor Company and CBS over the selection of plays and casting of this series. Once such example was the casting of Noel Coward in his two plays, *Blithe Spirit* and *This Happy Breed. Variety* had described the first as "a lackluster performance."[37] Hubbell Robinson commented that "Ford didn't feel we were giving them big enough shows with big enough stars." He stated "they did not want dramas, they wanted musicals, but there was not enough money for lavish musicals." So Ford cancelled out at the end of the season.

Worthington Miner and Kaiser Aluminum Hour

Worthington Miner finally got his chance to do hourly series drama that season. Since Pat Weaver brought him to NBC in the spring of 1952 his only assignments had been several half-hour series — *Medic,* dramatizations of medical case histories, and *Frontier,* a realistic type of Western drama about average people who went West. In July of 1956 he launched the *Kaiser Aluminum Hour* as the replacement for *Playwrights '56.* The show was produced by Unit Four Productions, of which Miner was the executive producer with three producer-directors who alternated in production: Fielder Cook of *Kraft Television Theater* and *Patterns* fame; George Roy Hill, also of *Kraft Television Theater,* known for his *A Night to Remember;* and Franklin Schaffner, formerly associated with *Studio One*. The series had a rather stormy life. On December 2 it was announced that Worthington Miner had resigned as executive producer of Unit Four Productions and by the end of January, Unit Four was officially ejected as the producing unit of the *Kaiser Aluminum Hour*. There had been public displays of differences between the sponsors and producers for several months. The Unit charged that the sponsor disapproved of several plays it wanted to produce.[38] In turn, the sponsor, through the Young and Rubicam Agency, indicated dissatisfaction with the plays that were produced. Some of the scripts that caused arguments were John Galsworthy's *Loyalties;* a topical drama on the Poznań trials; *Memphis by Morning* by Robert Alan Aurthur, dealing with Northern and Southern racial attitudes in an accident concerning a white driver and a black victim; *The Healer* by Loring Mandel, the story of a faith healer who loses and regains his faith; and *The Gathering* by Reginald Rose, which dealt with a family in an air raid with an O. Henry twist when it was discovered that the family portrayed was Russian and the air raid was in Moscow. Miner explained:

> We had a contract for an autonomous operation. But Mr. Kaiser wanted a happy show — everything comes out in the end. For example, after the Poznań Trials show he came into New York and raised hell and NBC backed us up. He then threatened to go to Washington — this was the beginning of some Senate investigations. You can't buck Henry Kaiser. He was going to have the kind of show he wanted.[39]

In resigning, Miner stated, "I realized then that network broadcasting of dramatic shows was doomed. I quit. Once the networks sacrificed control to advertisers, live drama was doomed." "Henry Kaiser," said Miner, "didn't want plays on topics such as the semitic problem." In contrast, he said "one of the things that made *Studio One* possible was that 90 percent of the disputes with Westingthouse were decided in favor of me." He exclaimed, "I could not have created that show otherwise!"[40]

At a meeting with the Young and Rubicam Agency and with Henry Kaiser himself, the Unit Four producers were told "to stay in the American non-controversial format."[41] Talent Associates, which produced the *Armstrong Circle Theater,* took over, but in the spring both Kaiser and the Armstrong accounts walked out on NBC. They theoretically did not wish to compete with CBS's *$64,000 Question* without a half-hour lead.

The Last Hurrahs

In December 1957 when *Studio One* joined *Climax* and *Playhouse 90* at CBS's Television City in Hollywood, television types in New York were destroyed by the news, and the opening production, "Brotherhood of the Bell," brought this *New York Times* comment: "Apprehensions over the fate of *Studio One* were fully justified . . . the show was pretentious mediocrity." By April Westinghouse announced it was replacing it with a filmed show after ten consecutive years on the air, and two days later NBC announced that *Kraft Television Theater* was cancelled. *Alcoa-Goodyear* and *Robert Montgomery Presents* had given up earlier.[42] An article on the eight year run of *Robert Montgomery Presents* in the *New Republic* in September 1957 claimed television had been wasting away for two years and had "suddenly given up the ghost." The author, Martin Luray, quoted Robert Montgomery in a depressing statement:

> Fifty-two productions a year is hard manual labor, but I have no feeling of relief that it is over. I feel kind of empty about the whole situation.[43]

While the 1957–58 season was the end for New York, Pat Weaver's "spectacular" concept still provided network programming with its chief claim to quality entertainment. The new *DuPont Show of the Month* on CBS, produced by Talent Associates, had several successes, the most exciting of which was an adaptation of *The Bridge of San Luis Rey*.[44] *Playhouse 90* returned on CBS, but it was the six *Hall of Fame* specials on NBC that captured the big headlines. *Hall of Fame* premiered with Marc Connelly's adaptation of his Pulitzer Prize play, *The Green Pastures*. There was an all–Negro cast of 60, headed by William Warfield as De Lawd, Eddie "Rochester" Anderson as Noah, and Cab Calloway as the King of Babylon. It was described as a magnificent achievement, done with taste, humor, and reverence.[45] The *Hall of Fame* production in March of an original, *Little Moon of Albans* by James Costigan, starring Julie Harris and Christopher Plummer, was also significant and won most of the Sylvania and Emmy awards, and the *Hallmark* series received the Peabody Award for the best television entertainment that season.[46]

One aspect of the change in network programming was that live television was no longer associated with "just" entertainment but with "quality" entertainment. This was unfortunate in terms of survival. It is best illustrated by *Producer's Showcase*'s most interesting performance of an Old Vic production of *Romeo and Juliet,* starring Claire Bloom and John Neville. It was a glorious 90 minutes and the *Times* review the morning after excitedly said: "To know that such supreme theatre was enjoyed in every city and village should give all concerned reason for pride and satisfaction."[47] But the following week the Trendex audience ratings for the show and its CBS competition were as follows:

	8–8:30	8:30–9	9–9:30
Romeo and Juliet	15.6	14.8	10.9
Burns and Allen	20.8		
Talent Scouts (Godfrey)		26.3	
I Love Lucy			41.6

The interpretation of these results was that *Romeo and Juliet* had had very few viewers in contrast to the rivals' attractions. *Variety* commented two days later: "Shakespeare doesn't pay off on television."[48] Gould was shocked at the attitude that NBC presumably had goofed in the competitive business of broadcasting and stated:

> I can't believe that anyone at NBC had expected *Romeo and Juliet* to make a good showing against Gracie Allen, Arthur Godfrey, and Lucille Ball. The rating services, however, make it appear as if NBC was deficient.... In their total impact they [the ratings] pose the ridiculous notion that *Romeo and Juliet* must be equated with *I Love Lucy* in terms of mass popularity. We do not equate Shakespeare in any other medium, as literature, as legitimate theatre (even in Classic Comics) with the popularity of Mike Hammer.[49]

For years, the networks, the critics, the producers and directors, had all preached that the immediacy, the spontaneity of live television was its most important characteristic. The errors on a taped or filmed show can be rectified. Thus to many of the people involved, film was a more technical medium, less artistic, less satisfying. And in the end it was a mistake to equate live broadcast with quality. Talk shows are still successful on television because they give the illusion of immediacy and spontaneity.

The published lamentations coming out of New York when live television died would fill several volumes. But some of the comments in interviews with the major players were more interesting. Miner was brutal and blunt:

> Hollywood meant bad crap. It meant stars and bad scripts and money. You practically have to get out of Hollywood to make a fine picture. If they can foul their own nest, they certainly can ruin television.[50]

Edmund Rice was also specific:

> Yes, film was ruled out by the economies of broadcasting. If it had been kept out we could have developed something really great—now it is a bastard medium.[51]

Albert McCleery has already been quoted on the film magnates' boycott of television, and while he was a convert to Hollywood production facilities, he was no fan of Hollywood producers:

> It would be interesting if someone would do a psychological study of what was happening in Hollywood. They thought it was a fad! These were the same people that goofed up on the talkies and tried to hold back radio.
>
> There's an arrogance about the networks that's frightening. They are like the feudal lords on the hill. I've got it—no one else can have it—King of the Mountain! They look askance at the idea that this is a public utility.
>
> When you look at it—what is a network? No industry ever had such a small capital outlay with such a large profit.
>
> The nets say they give the people what they want. We had slavery—it was the will of the majority. But it wasn't good for us.
>
> Sarnoff and the networks resent the performers and producers. They brag about balance in programming. This is the devil's excuse—a cover for crap. They point to the news. We will end up the best informed, uncultured slobs in the world![52]

Fred Coe blamed ABC:

> Ironically, you would think the more competition you got would help. But ABC jumped in and did not compete at the level of CBS and NBC. They were like the Giants and the Dodgers and ABC was a bush leaguer. Both of the big networks had third rate shows, but both were conscious of their public responsibility. They were going to make television artistically important—even while competing with one another. ABC came in and took advantage of this competition and introduced what I call their "horse-ass" operas, their 42nd Street side shows, their Disneyland public relations shows; and they lowered television. They made it into a side show. They didn't care about anything but the ratings. NBC and CBS had had enough pride to attempt to do

something worthwhile. ABC entered at the cheapest level of competition.[53]

The commercial intrusion of the advertiser has always received the bulk of television's criticism. Hubbell Robinson put it this way:

> If it is a morass of mediocrity, a weekly shambles of violence and villainy, a belt-line assemblage of repetitive inanity, it is because a vast number of those Americans passively accept it that way. They watch it; they buy the products it peddles.[54]

We quoted the eminent critic and novelist John Crosby early in this book, as he "bid farewell to TV" in a column in the *Los Angeles Mirror*. He stated "Television isn't awful. Awful things are fun to write about. . . . But *Rawhide* isn't really that awful. It's a bore." He continues in this same column in 1960 with a point of view that is quite different from Hubbell Robinson's:

> I am appalled that this great medium of information and education is so totally dedicated to utter vacuity. Don't be misled by the professional apologists that this is all television can afford to do or all the public wants of it. The people want and deserve something much better than they're getting. As for what TV can afford, all I know is that it annually grosses $600,000,000 and for that kind of money it ought to do better than "Pete and Gladys."[55]

Last Words

Television is a broadcast medium. Unlike the producing agencies of motion pictures, television stations lease their privilege to broadcast only as long as they "broadcast in the public interest, convenience and necessity." The fundamental concept remains that broadcasting has a basic purpose of which entertainment is only a part. But the reality is that entertainment is its *proximate purpose.* The ultimate reality is that the idea behind television is *not to entertain,* but to sell sponsors' products.

In 1961 a 35-year-old Chicago law partner of Adlai Stevenson's named Newton Minow, became FCC chairman. This courageous man dared to stand up before the moguls of the broadcast industry and the bosses of Madison Avenue and tell them to their faces what was wrong with television. His castigation of the industry was unprecedented. It had never been done before. He described the majority of television shows as a "vast wasteland." "I did not come to Washington to idly observe the squandering of the public's air waves," he said, describing them as a "precious natural resource."[56]

Though it is true that the networks immediately began mending their political fences and public image and featured more news and information programs, the prime viewing hours were slow to change. The viewing audiences appeared to get more sophisticated in the 1970s and miniseries such as *Roots* were tremendously successful. Cable and satellites brought more choice to the audiences of the 1980s but because of the twin pressures of *time* and *money,* the melancholy fact is that television is seldom as good as it could be.

Appendix I
Memorandum from NBC's
Pat Weaver, 1955*

MEMORANDUM ON NBC MATINEE
TO: Jane Murray
FROM: Pat Weaver

July 4, 1955

This is a memorandum to all concerned based on our decision to go ahead this fall with hour dramas, different each day, from 3:00 to 4:00 on NBC under the over-all direction of Al McCleery.

This latest drama plan has a lot of predecessor ideas which can enrich and stimulate the new final NBC matinee pattern and I want to recap some of them and also point out why I agreed to make this tremendous gamble on the 3- to 4-hour plan.

First of all we have some immediate difficulties like the P&G acceptance of the plan which if not handled properly can really

*This is dictated material provided by Jane Murray, and reprinted here by permission. It is typical of the rambling, free-wheeling memo style of the creative genius, Pat Weaver. As president of NBC, he was responsible for much of television as we know it today — the Today Show, the Tonight Show, programming of specials, the magazine concept of advertising, and so on. Albert McCleery, who produced Matinee Theater, said of this memo: "It was a beautiful thing. We did not fully understand it but it called for the birth of a great new theater, a springboard for the great actors, directors and playwrights of the future."

jeopardize the possibility of going ahead. We also have problems of handling our talent and we have the problems of budget that are still being estimated with a high degree of hunch. In other words, the present figure for five hour dramas a week, in color from Hollywood under Al's direction, are not as precise as we would like to have them.

More important, however, is my feeling that the five hours a week are valuable in part in themselves but more so because of the tremendous control they give NBC over the planned development of dramatic production in television. I think that the possibilities as I will outline them that can be done once a great drama machine is underway, are so exhilarating that we must go forward with the plan.

Many of the points made require individuals in NBC to use judgment and common sense as they figure out how they can best fit into this over-all philosophy, and how their present assignment can be extended or changed to make them helpful in the new dramatic project.

It is hard to spell out the impact of any new project on each member of NBC and even each department. It is presumed by me that the various executives responsible will, themselves, attempt to analyze the effect of the project on themselves and their departments in an effort to modify their practices so that they can be more helpful to the new project. As an example, Sales and Legal know that the whole trend of the business is toward the right of way of NBC to take back time periods for occasional broadcasts and for regularly scheduled monthly broadcasts and, therefore, everything they should be doing should be making it more easy for us to accomplish an end which will see 15 or 20 percent of our time each week given over to special broadcasts. This is an example of what I mean of departments thinking ahead to the impact of what we are doing on what they should be doing.

As you will see when we get to drama, the impact is particularly directed at the whole program development operation, and the writing development plan. But it does include talent and all nighttime producers really are affected by some of the possibilities, as outlined below.

Originally, when we started in television, and soaps began to rear their ugly heads, there was a big conflict between some of us who felt that television was going to be different enough from radio so that the old technique would not work; the old soap opera radio technique would not work, and that we should try for stories more complete in themselves from day to day because of the higher absorption and the tension demands of television over radio. And the group who felt strongly that the radio formula in daytime soap operas, as in other entertainment, would be effective in television. Because of the great experience that the latter group had, in general we have gone along with them. Furthermore, in the case of CBS, from twelve to one, over a long period of time and aided greatly by bad shows on NBC, the soap opera block has been effective. However, even there, we are told by P&G, that the difference in hit quality in the individual attractions is far far more important than it ever was in radio, and that a bad show, or one that does not catch hold after a hit, will not carry its audience as it did in radio.

Meanwhile, a soap opera block on NBC from 11 to 12 did not get off the ground. After P&G swung the famous double four to five or ten million dollars worth of business to CBS, at the beginning of '54, we countered with a three to five soap opera block to see if we could hold their business and were successful in holding a part of it with this new plan, which represented a straight concession to their thinking on our part. This, as you know, has not been successful, although 4:00 to 5:00 is not unsuccessful as 3:00 to 4:00. The soaps finally gave way, earlier this year, to entertainment programs, personalities, and we are still testing them. In the case of Ted Mack and the new Bill Goodwin show we will be placing hit personality shows in time periods other than 3:00 to 4:00 and if these shows have impact we will keep them. In other words, there is no reason to feel that Bill Goodwin is thrown off before he starts because we have time periods in the daytime which are not successfully programmed and we have time periods that the stations would give us if we had successful programming to put in — at least many of them have told us so and this includes the 2:00 to 3:00 afternoon time period.

Following, however, the soaps not taking off too strongly, even on CBS, the next move of the daytime drama argument was to find a middle way between the soap opera technique of continuing stories and the technique of a story complete in itself each day, which was the competitor. This is going way back five years when the proposal was made to do five half-hour shows with a story complete in itself each day, as against two soap operas back-to-back. This was followed by a compromise in which the five half-hours each day would all revolve around characters that were firm for the whole locale of the shows — in other words, there would be one doctor and one drugstore and one lawyer, and so forth, who would appear in different stories, but the stories themselves would be individual.

This compromise was succeeded by another one called *Home Town,* where four soap operas to take care of conventional buying demands were put back-to-back but within a framework of a town, as in the half-hour strip, with the same characters running through. This was an exciting plan — an excellent plan — and with proper backing probably would have worked. However, in the time between *Home Town* and *Today* there has been a turn away from conventional soap opera and today we would have to evaluate *Home Town* as against the new five-hour plan and the new dimensions of television — and it certainly has great advantages to go with the present new hour-drama-daily plan.

The most recent of a number of other dramatic programs was the idea of running movies, either the same movie — a great A picture — re-presented to the public for the first time out of theatres and on television — the same picture to be played five days a week to get the cumulative audience so that everybody, in effect, in America would see the movie. This plan, and many variations which included five different pictures a week and repeats and all the other combinations and permutations, was finally abandoned for money reasons about six weeks ago.

Additional plans, including two projects outlined by Joey Chester a few weeks ago, brought up the final creative catalyzation(?) which ended in the proposals by McCleery for the five hours once a week.

The important thing to remember when you have a project finally agreed upon that has a real long history, is that many different values are present here and they must all be taken in to consideration and made to work for the over-all project. If we play our cards right this project can not only be a great success that returns to NBC its three o'clock leadership and therefore takes care of us for the afternoon, because a 3:00 to 4:00 success means a 4:00 to 5:00 success and helps us even in our new conflicts with the Mouse at five o'clock.

But it is unlikely that five cameo-style stories, done with the budget that we have discussed, will turn this trick on sheer merit. It's possible that this could happen but it is certainly not what we will gamble on. The money is too great to let Al, without help, attempt to solve the problem by the sheer genius of his creative powers.

Rather, we should consider NBC and its enterprises as a funnel through which will flow to the 3:00 to 4:00 daytime five-hours-a-week, a flood of properties, artists, stories, ideas, opportunities and advantages which will give Al a range of powers far beyond anything that he could afford or could have harnessed into his own immediate producing organization. I will be more specific about this on the other side.

First of all, Al will have a studio in Hollywood where, as I understand it, only the Milton Berle color programs will dispossess him, barring urgent and important operations not now foreseen.

I firmly believe that nothing is better looking than big faces in color and that from 3:00 to 4:00 across the country if the color sets are showing heads—that there will be a tremendously good reaction in our over-all color problems. As a matter of fact, the show that I will never forget as the one that really made me believe in color, was Vice President Barkley being interviewed by Earl Godwin. That was the early color show that made me really get sent on color, because I had not realized until that time that the real impact of color was showing you real people as they really are. I had thought of it more as a technicolor device that would show Mounties riding in with red coats on, and all the rest that's really the superficial aspects of color presentation. The real secret of color as a powerful weapon is that it shows you the real world as it really is. This includes theatre too, but theatre is only a part of it.

This studio should be organized and rehearsal schedules set up in such a way that the basic hour shows are done on a schedule that makes sense economically in terms of the union calls for the crews, and so forth, and the shows should, in general, be developed to fit that commercial pattern. I know Al understands this because I've already discussed it with him and he has plans for certain kinds of lighting positions, and so forth, which, in the big studio, he can handle and leave standing, so that we will be able to do this tremendously complicated and expensive job without any feeling that it is being done on an economical scale. This also brings up the size of the studio which, in any kind of camera work that wants space attributes, can get the tremendous deep shots available in the new color studio in Burbank. And for those frankly experimental dramas that will be done from time to time in any such volume project as we're discussing here—the Burbank color studio will really challenge the ingenuity and imaginations of writers and producers.

Without in any way attempting to give priority I will now describe in item forms things that should be done and harnessed into the overall NBC matinee.

When major stars are approached for big deals that involve substantial commitments on our side, and this involves not only our spectaculars but even the hour-dramas and as a matter of coordination through Len Hole's program and talent development operation, of the buying practices of the *Robert Montgomery, Fred Coe, Kraft Theater, Lux Theater, Pontiac, Armstrong Theater* axis (access?). When a star makes a deal for a show, every effort should be made to get the star to agree to do one daytime show, perhaps with a rerun right so that we would get two uses out of it. This brings up bookkeeping and until we know more about the possibility of getting the star, it is hard to be specific. The reason that we give to the stars is frankly that we are trying to upgrade dramatic entertainment in the daytime for women and that their name will add prestige and lustre to the operation and do a good thing for themselves and for us and for the theatre and television generally. This sell may fall on deaf ears with the agents, but I think it can be done, certainly in enough cases, to make it worthwhile. Again the premise would be that artist A signs for a Monday night spectacular and agrees to do a daytime cameo-type one-hour drama with a single repeat right included in the original deal by kinescope and this is to be in at the convenience and with script approval, etc. Obviously here we are trying to get, over the course of the year, enough big names with enough appearances to have a quality feeling to the series.

In the writing development plan, certain basic stories and myths and classics and properties in the public domain can be selected, either by Al or by others in the development operation, and assigned to young writers, giving the specifications needed from our production point of view. As for instance largely cameo-style and with limitations on the number of actors, etc. The adaptations written by these people, and perhaps 10 or 20 could write an adaptation of the same show, would be available for Al's use. It would give an immediate exposure position for the writing development plan to have as great a need of material as will be forthcoming with *NBC Matinee*.

The elements of theatre that have been successful from time to time should be studied carefully by all of us with the hope that we could take semi-risks on the *NBC Matinee* by trying things that we would never wish to try over all, but as part of the operation we are not afraid to try. For instance, back before the first World War the matinee idol was a great feature of the legitimate stage and later in silent movies there were a number of men who achieved the status of matinee idols. This has more or less gone out with the talkies and the theatre of late but as I believe Walter Kerr once outlined in one of his provocative columns, the matinee idol still has a lot of power left in him. If we were to go through all of the actors available to us and pick the one that we thought could be made into a matinee idol, because of personal magnetism and personality and so forth, and if we were to work on his personal style, accentuating it in degree and nuances in order to actually tailor-make for ourselves a matinee idol, and if we were then to have vehicles written that would bring out these qualities in the way and the swagger, if that is the quality, or lack of diction if that is the quality, that this kind of star-building operation requires. The matinee idol is a good three-show attempt over a 2- or 3-month period to see if we have anything either in the plan or in the particular idol that we get—we may have to clast that idol and get a new one. It reminds me that iconoclast means image-destroyer, so this is an idolclast, an idol-destroyer.

This is a little bit different from star-building in general but certainly with five hours a week of presentation together with the six hour nighttime dramas we now have enough production under our control or where we can make it in self interest worth the while of J. Walter Thompson and others to cooperate with us in getting stars and material and so forth. We can now move out really on a star-building basis. When we put Grace Kelly on the air in the Michael Arlen show *Cads and Scoundrels* back five years and some months ago, it was obvious that she was really something. But if we signed her it would do us very little good, as CBS found out when it signed some dramatic stars of great promise and then really could do nothing with them. But that's quite a different thing from today when we will have direct control of five hours a week, very close control of a few more, and certainly persuasive power over a few more. A new Grace Kelly comes along and we should be able, through the NBC Talent Department, to sign her on a guarantee basis of some kind with agreements by the nighttime hours as well as AI, to use the girl often enough to make her guarantee and of course she gains by the promotion and the exploitation that we will give her to make her a star as rapidly as possible and that is far faster than is available to movies.

When I say a girl I mean a girl or boy or old man or anything else that anybody believes can be made into a star.

I also mean of course that the same type of operation that you use for making stars is available for writers. There is no reason to believe that as we find good writers that we cannot, with some sort of a base guarantee, have them exclusively available to us. There is enough range between our nighttime and daytime dramas to keep them busy.

Similarly when we get to program development of shows we have now suddenly a new situation with five hours of dramatic production a week directly controlled by us. We can go out and purchase a novel that we know would be a good television show and have two or three adaptations written because we now have a place to play that show if we do not place it in our nighttime presentations. The whole question of buying material and having properties developed for television takes on an entirely different prospect with the beginning of the *NBC Matinee*. All people in production, in talent, in program development, should think about this new prospect and devise ways and means that the additional production that will be going out on our facilities be harnessed for the good of developing better material, better writers, giving actors more of a chance to become stars, etc.

I mentioned the matinee idol as a line of attack. A similar one . . . [end of record].

If you were to think about somebody who could do this, like Spencer Tracy, or somebody who would do this, like Hume Cronyn, and could, as well, you will follow my thought. You would write at least six, or perhaps more, different characterizations for the actor. He wouldn't be made up in each of the characterizations and a motion picture made of a montage of these as a sort of promotion plan and device — an actor-building device emphasizing the actor's ability to act in various characterizations, as against appealing as a matinee idol does. Each of the shows would be Tracy or Cronin or whoever in a role that is precisely defined in some way. The shows themselves would of course be character delineations in large part but then a great deal of television is going to be that anyway. The power of the actor in the big hit form is without any question overpowering. This again gets down to writing by direction. In other words, you get writers in and you say "Writer, I want you to write me a story about Spencer Tracy in a character in each succeeding generation from the time of the beginning of the United States until now, or roughly, let us say, 3 to 100 years so that you would have six characterizations including one that would be slightly in the future." Then the writer would come back and say I have them here. The first one is one of the founding fathers of the country, the second one is a pioneer in the early days of the move to the Ohio Valley, the third one is a southern gentleman in the pre–Civil War period, the fourth one is in the war, and so forth — and you would pick — you would then build something that would have real meat for the star and would trap the star into being willing to do the plan. You would also give an exciting over-all pattern for the public and the people, something to talk about, something to look forward to. This kind of attempt is quite separate from the matinee idol or even the star-building attempts, but again indicates the tremendous flood of new thinking that can emanate from mass production of drama.

One of the things that I have been strongly urging for some time but without too much success, is to attempt to take a great basic attraction such as a play or a book or a movie or a public domain theme and instead of deciding to do a series — the old idea — or to do a one-shot — which is our new idea and we are now getting pretty well into the firmament — that we take the middle way, which is to say that *Showboat* or *Gone with the Wind* or *Roger's Rangers* or *Captain Horatio Hornblower* — any major attraction already known largely to the American public — but instead of doing a series or instead of doing a one-shot, one plans to do a series of episodic one-shots but with the same characters, locale, feeling and style, except that each one has a sub-plot that becomes complete in itself in the single hour. For instance, if one were doing in these daytime dramas, stories about Scarlett O'Hara, each of the episodes would not have to follow the original book at all but would merely be based upon the characters, the locale, the spirit and style of the book and would be complete-in-themselves shows without any cliff-hanger techniques. This obviously couldn't be an older idea. Movies have been running Hardy families and Maisie stories from the beginning. Before them came books who kept presenting new adventures of the similar artist or a succeeding episode of a family's life, etc. Nonetheless, I don't believe that we are consciously attempting to find good basic characterizations and locales of stories and then thinking not in terms of an adaptation but as a series of let us say a dozen hour shows based upon *Mama*, if it hadn't been made into a serial, or *Gone with the Wind* or any of the basic attractions as mentioned above.

This again merely indicates another approach to the whole field of material, another approach to the whole field of roles for stars.

This also brings up the possibility of Al doing a stock company idea such as we have discussed elsewhere, but again where the possibilities of the stock company not being as good as it should have always held us back from doing very much about it. The closest to it being done is the Montgomery summer show.

But if one of the five days a week for a 13 week period, at some given time, was to be devoted to the NBC repertory theatre, with seven or eight good actors agreeing to take a 13 week job, Al could then present a real rep-theatre type presentation which is, of course, tremendously helpful, particularly to the actors. How good it is for audience is a question that would depend upon the actors and the material and the production. There is no reason to believe that it could not be excellent theatre, and, therefore, get big audiences. But, it again, in my thinking, is mainly as an extremely valuable weapon in developing our medium; training actors; broadening the range of product offered the public, finding a way in which classics can be adapted for television and used successfully, even though presented individually and by themselves and without explanation they might not be fully understandable to the great audiences.

I cannot drop the classics without mentioning one long-time hope that I only submit for the record. If we have the color remote unit in California it is just possible that Al might want to do an adaptation of one of the classics in his series and, of course, the Greek Theatre in Griffith Park would be an ideal location for such a drama. Again, in the kind of a project that I can foresee, being behind the actual NBC matinee, I can easily foresee this not only being done, but being so promoted that it would become a highly reported and looked forward to and done with a large audience in great success. This is because I believe that the people will always watch something that they are not interested in if they have been sold on the idea that it is valuable or rewarding or inherently good, or in general have a feeling of prestige associated with it, a feeling that if they do like it it reflects credit on them, and if they don't like it it reflects lack of knowledge on their side. In any event, in a range of products such as can be offered on *NBC Matinee,* including classics presented outside the Burbank Studio, can be considered. The money is something else again. I don't know about the cost of doing a Greek Theatre presentation with the outside unit. But here again I recommend to the financial men, as I have always, and as I know they have responded to nobly in many parts, it does us no good to have expensive equipment that is not being used because the price placed upon it is so high that none of our own producers will use it. The proper thing to do is to get the actual cost of the use in order to get it used and made into an indispensable tool by the producers and then eventually the cost of the optional instrument will become more and more non-optional and basic.

I am saying that if the color remote unit is priced at full price and is not used, the mistake is not in the Program Department, but in the department that puts the price on it.

Certainly, the purchase of stories for television, either already published or one-page originals, as the movies did for so long and has been recommended to us from time to time, is a must that should be harnessed in at once in the program development operations of the network now that Al is going ahead with the five hours a week. Originals, a couple of pages long should be set up on some basis, announcements should be made, stories should come in in which the writer of the original gets a small fee and a second payment if used, and a percentage of the residuals with the adapter. This is most important. The use of short originals in Hollywood was extremely successful and it can be even more successful to us. This, again, is something that must be set up organizationally, but the responsibility of it first of all is in Len Hole's department, because he is supposed to be coordinating all of the activities in the procurement and development of programs and talent and material.

When it comes to writer development, one of the great areas where you can find out whether somebody has imagination and knowledge and insight is to assign classics for adaptation. If you take the works of any of the lesser known classical writers, including the writers of antiquity, and have young writers take a whirl at adaptations, I think it will be demonstrated whether or not they have major talent or whether they are not really ready for the major challenge. I am thinking of Terrence and then the earlier European writers, but not, of course, Shakespeare. I'm not at all sure that some of the great classics that nobody sees anymore couldn't be used for adaptation. But if you take writers, particularly if you have a young team of writers, then you give them Marlowe or Molière or an early novel by Dodge and set them to work, bringing in an hour show adaptation built on the character and plot that has been delivered to them, I think it will be remarkable what you may find. Both ways.

Despite the fact that the budget may preclude music in a conventional sense, I think we should seriously consider the possibility of using music on these shows that is distinctive, like the "Third Man" music with the zither. I don't know quite how we could handle this but it is a question for us to seriously work on. It might be well worth the money to have even an unusual 6-piece combo that would have available to it recorded music as well as their own live compositions and work out a 5-day-week scoring arrangement that would get the style of music in to help carry the drama and give it the feeling of freshness and individuality that I know it can have.

On music, one obvious line of thought is to take the instrumentation that we generally associate with the period. If you're doing historical drama and use that, thus the harpsichord takes care of whole period and you can get to the classics with a lute-like presentation and the East comes up with a flute and Africa with a drum, etc., etc. In modern times you have a muted trumpet for the '20s and for the story about a child you have a harmonica and for the story about a young artist you can have a recorder, and so forth. If it's the story about an engineer you can even have a music that really was an instrument pretending to be sound, as a sort of music synthesizer—noise.

Music is one of the corollary attributes of this over-all project that will give it the feeling of importance and size and scope and excitement that we want. We don't want to sneak hour-dramas and get the word out that they're cameo-styled to save money and that the whole thing is something other than it is. What it is is a tremendous and exhilarating dramatic project that has more promise in it than anything we have ever done, as far as bringing maturity and scope and range to the story-telling part of our medium. This feeling should also be present in the finalization of the name and in the presentation of the opening and the close. Here, space, scope, sweep, mobility, bigness, stature, prestige—these are the qualities that we want to get as we go to what then becomes good drama done largely in big heads because it is the story of people and we are stressing people in the kind of material that we will deliver. We must get cracking on real projection, particularly if color is going to bring up some problems, because that is one of the ways that Al can get more extension in his presentation.

One of the avenues for volume production of drama is the subject matter pattern which directs again the kind of material you try to find, the kind you try to have written for you and kind that you try to promote as an entity so that the individual dramas are aided and supported by something bigger than themselves.

I am dictating this on the Fourth of July, so naturally I think of patriotism as a basic thought. One could, during this particular week, run five hour-dramas that take five variations on the theme of either the founding of our Republic, or the theme of patriotism or something. Similarly at Christmas one can do five Christmas stories during the week and by proper long-range planning and projection and the obtaining of a title and an idea and a trailer, that can be used for promotion in radio and television, one can make a real event of this series of presentations on the Christmas theme. This again is another avenue to demonstrate the kind of thinking that all of us can do to provide further richness and body to this essentially great plan.

In the program development side I think that we would have an interesting project if we went out to the amateur dramatic, or professional dramatic, groups across the country and we said that if they would send in a story outline for a show that they believe would make a good one-hour drama on film, and if they would point out why they could handle that story — in other words, if the University of Denver or Utah, or someplace in the Rockies, had a story that would be shot on location with horses or in the mines or on the ski slopes, and if they laid out a story that, in other words, had a real grass roots Americana feeling, we would consider sending to the stories we selected, say the two leads, a director and a cameraman who would complete the job with the local community. In other words, a 50-minute motion picture would be made having in mind the *NBC Matinee* theatre as the distribution point and we would do one from Taos, New Mexico and we would do one from La Jolla, California and we would do one from Buffalo, New York and so forth, but each would be particularly important to do on location because of some values and that they would be essentially the product of the local area but in order to give positive smooth performance we would step in with a couple of the leading roles and a couple of creative people and the funds to carry it through to a conclusion. However, even in this case we might make exceptions and let groups carry the whole thing through, if they require it. But this is again another field now not being touched that could provide a rich flow of material to us or at least there is a chance that this could happen.

It is planned of course that the television series be live for *NBC Matinee*. Nonetheless, we must remember the possibility of replaying nighttime kinescopes and figure out how much this would cost and see if we can plan for precontracting with rights to get those costs down so that they could be used in this series. This is in addition to getting script rights for use, specifically where possible for a second run in conjunction with the first run at a lower price on the basis that it would either help the first run or build the property to do a second version of it in the period before or after the nighttime show.

We must also remember that five hours a week is a lot of hours and that it may well be for budget and other reasons that four would be preferable with the fifth being a motion picture production or kinescope production. It might even be that Al would want to have one show a week taken out of production and being supplied to him or that a backlog be built for vacation of his entire troupe and staff by having two weeks of filmed programs at some point. In any event, this is not the time to decide to cut down on any possible sources of hour-shows when we are about to add five daytime to our already-added-to nighttime list.

Therefore, such ideas as could be done in kinescope even though in black and white and even though not in Hollywood, should be worked on and considered. But I am thinking less of our NBC people doing additional shows for Al, than I am thinking of the opportunities to use our development money to bring new products in and to experiment with hours, which, if they do not turn out, we throw in the ashcan, but if they do turn out we have a place to use them on the *NBC Matinee*. Along the lines of the above suggestion of community groups there are also small task force groups who could do pictures on a shoestring. This is particularly true where the pictures really are based on either locale or basic job or a historical period or something. For instance, one could do a complete Indian story in the woods with Indians if it were a strong personal story and done in a semi-documentary way and done by a little group of three or four people who were devoted to their mission and took their equipment and a small amount of money and just went and came back with a 50-minute story about Indians. This could be the Indian story with the big "I wish I'd said that" finish.

The Kon-Tiki film is in a way an example of what I'm talking about. Here we sit in New York with our program development money and in romps John Sutherland with an idea and a young writer-photographer which involves chartering a two-masted schooner for a month in the Bahamas to do a story to be shot on the boat and one tired cay. Providing this is not very much money that they're talking about, it seems to me that we could very well finance it, hope for the best, because we know that if it is a good result we can use it on *NBC Matinee.* If we were to do it today with only the nighttime shows as availabilities, we would probably give them a great deal more money but we would expect a great deal more picture. If they're doing it on a shoestring I think that the chances are that it would be either a good picture or not, not because of funds but because of the essential idea and the people doing it. The difference between a $10,000 advance and a $50,000 advance to a group of zealots who are going to come back with footage is more in the quality of the zealots and their idea than in the difference of $40,000. I think.

This has another great advantage in that if you had little foreign-intrigue-type companies romping around the world doing stories on location in which most of the story that was shot outside with 16 with voice-over and narrative technique and in which your basic sound-on-film footage was kept to a very low part of the over-all, to save money, you might come up with an occasional show which would be a source of real extension for the series because of being originals shot in the faraway places with all of the glamour and romance that one gets from that sort of thing. I am sure, for instance, that any good photographer and writer could go to the Himalayan Massif with Tenczig and do a story that was essentially a narration of the mountains with stock footage and the footage that he would shoot, but yet had enough in it to make a good 50-minute show that would appeal to the people. Whether this could be done for a few thousand dollars or not, I have no idea. But between the Indian movie companies and desire of the other governments to help, and our government to help, it seems to me that ingenuity and good management could make a few hard dollars and a great promotion device go a long way toward bringing exciting film material to this country where the real star is the foreign country rather than the story or the actors. This, again, falls into the Len Hole development area primarily.

In the other version of movies, I was thinking of the success those fellows in Hollywood had who made very cheap pictures by concentrating on a profession or a vocation that was exciting and had a lot of nuts and bolts. Pictures that were at least full of character for people who had never seen them before. It is a way of escaping the necessity for having a strong story and even good characterizations. Locale makes up for a lot.

If we were to take the strangest occupations, like Fred Allen used to have on his program. If you build a story about a man who puts boats in bottles, you have something going for you almost from the beginning. You may even have a finish in which you're in the bottle looking out.

Revivals of great attractions is an obvious part of our overall plan that should be under consideration. So should an extension of the great success that Al had with biographies on *Hallmark*.

If we're going for women we must have ratings or we are not successful. And, therefore, it seems to me that somebody who really knows not only good drama, but good soap opera, should sit down or be added to Al's group or in an advisory capacity to it to talk to the great all time daytime soap writers with the thought of having them use their 25 years of material to single out the strongest sequences that they used to run over a 15 week period, with the thought that those could be constructed into single dramas, perhaps even starring the same cast that originally played out the role. I'm saying here that the form of the soap opera, since the characterizations are well established and the plots are extensive, could lend itself to the occasional hour production form mentioned above. Irma Philips might well become a ten-show-a-year writer, starting out with the basic shows that she has already written, now adapted and revised for our television shows, using, to begin with, the basic characters that she used before and as she becomes familiar with what's cooking, moving on to new triumphs of sentiment.

We must remember of course that our shows basically must have the same kind of appeal that, in large part, we find in the soap operas and the original Kate Smith show and in the other shows that we do have. I believe that nighttime quality will get huge audiences but I also believe that when we go for some of the specialized things I have been discussing we can only do so on the basis that our substantial diet from day to day is strong stories of interest to women, well written and well done. That is the basic stratum on which we will build our project. This is of course obvious but I'm repeating it because I'm about to close, I hope.

Even as we talk about star-building with this project, let us not forget that we have a vehicle for star-using here. We have rights with the Phil Harris' and Imogene Cocas and the Paul Gilberts, the younger element who are coming up, all of whom will learn from work in television and all of whom probably can be persuaded that performances in this kind of a show will be good for them in the sense that they will learn a lot and yet they are not taking the gamble of being sure that they were very strong, as they would have to be if they went on at night.

Also in the star-maker field, we have the advantage with volume of being able to get exclusive deals with major movie and theatrical talent. Incidentally, an extension of this would get us back to one of the old hometown—prehometown plans, which was that we would sign up seven or eight well-known stars, movie and theatrical stars, who would agree to be in an NBC stock company, and who would support each other in minor roles because they would be supported in major roles in an agreed-upon series of plays before any of them signed up. This is to take care of billing and jealousy and the rest of it. It's possible that a nighttime-daytime parlay could be worked out where this could then be accomplished. Needless to say, it would be a great promotion project and is well worth, again, the study of the coordinating committee.

Motion picture scripts which stack the files and originals in all the studios and in all the agents' offices suddenly have a new box office from NBC with the need for five hour-dramas a week. Let us remember however that our stuff is as good as theirs, in general, and that we don't need to buy their "Ivanhoe" when you can buy Scott for 25 cents in any drugstore. This goes for nearly all the really great material that's available. Most of the other stuff is actually filler that they use just as we do and there's no use buying their filler—we can buy their hits and they can buy our hits but we might easily develop our own filler, on both sides. Nonetheless, we should not avoid the embrace of Hollywood, if they are willing to deal on a reasonable basis. [END OF RECORDS]

Appendix II
A Sample of the
Growth and Demise of
Live Television Drama

The following lists of live television drama present two sample weeks of network drama: the first full week of December and the first full week of March in 1948–49, 1955–56 and the final two seasons, 1957–58 and 1958–59.

These lists show that in 1948–49 there were five or six live dramas a week. By 1955–56 the count had risen to 15 or so, and the format dominated prime time television. In 1957–58 there were still eight live shows a week but when the five-times-a-week *Matinee Theater* went off the air the numbers dropped to two shows a week and one of them, *Playhouse 90,* was occasionally on tape. By the fall of 1959 they were gone forever.

The 1948–49 Season

December 3–9, 1948

SUNDAY

  ABC: *Actor's Studio* (½ hour), "The Night the Ghost Got In" with Nydia Weston.

  CBS: (*Film Theater* this week alternates with *Ford Theatre.*)

  NBC: *Philco Television Playhouse* (hour), "Suspect" with Ruth Chatterton.

MONDAY
  NBC: *Chevrolet Tele-Theater* (½ hour), "Close Quarters" with
        Barry Nelson.

WEDNESDAY
  NBC: *Kraft Television Theater* (hour), "The Flashing Stream."

March 4-10, 1949

SUNDAY
  ABC: *Actor's Studio* (½ hour), "Joe McMiveen's Atomic Machine"
        with Don Hammer, Billy Redfield.
  CBS: *Studio One* (hour), "Julius Caesar" with William Post, Jr.,
        Philip Bourneuf (alternates with *Ford Theater*).
  NBC: *Philco Television Playhouse* (hour), "The Druid Circle"
        with Leo J. Carroll.

MONDAY
  NBC: *Chevrolet Tele-Theater* (½ hour), "Mr. Bell's Creation"
        with Janet Blair.
        Colgate Theater (½ hour), "The Florist Shop" with Ruth
        Gilbert.

WEDNESDAY
  NBC: *Kraft Television Theater* (hour), "Arrival of Kitty" with
        Gage Clarke.

The 1955-56 Season

December 4-10, 1955

SUNDAY
  NBC: *Alcoa-Goodyear Hour* (hour), "The Trees" by Jerome Ross.

MONDAY
  NBC: *Matinee Theater* (hour), "Arrowsmith" by Sinclair Lewis.
        Robert Montgomery Presents (hour), "Lucifer" by J.H.
        Howells.
  CBS: *Studio One* (hour), "Blow-Up at Cortland."

TUESDAY
NBC: *Matinee Theater* (hour), "Passing Strange" by E. Jack Neuman.
Playwrights '56 (hour), "The Sound and the Fury" by William Faulkner; alternates with *Armstrong Circle Theater.*

WEDNESDAY
NBC: *Matinee Theater* (hour), "For These Services."
Kraft Television Theater (hour), "Lady Ruth" by Jack Paritz.
CBS: *U.S. Steel Hour* (hour), "Edward, My Son" by Robert Morley.

THURSDAY
NBC: *Matinee Theater* (hour), "Cordially with Bombs."
Lux Video Theater (hour), "Suspicion" with Kim Hunter.
CBS: *Climax* (hour), "The Passport."
ABC: *Star Tonight* (½ hour), "Nightmare by Day."

FRIDAY
NBC: *Matinee Theater* (hour), "The Whiteoak."

March 4-10, 1956

SUNDAY
NBC: *Alcoa-Goodyear Hour* (hour), "Man on Fire" by Melvin Wald and Jack Jacobs starring Tom Ewell and Ed Begley.
CBS: *Front Row Center* (hour), "Innocent Witness" with Margaret O'Brien and Dean Stockwell.

(That Sunday the ABC Film Festival featured George Bernard Shaw's "Caesar and Cleopatra" with Vivian Leigh and Claude Rains. It was also produced that week on *Producer's Showcase* — see immediately below.)

MONDAY
NBC: *Matinee Theater* (hour), "Dinner at Antoine's" adapted by Samuel Taylor from the novel by Frances P. Keyes.
Producer's Showcase (1½ hours), "Caesar and Cleopatra" by George Bernard Shaw, starring Claire Bloom, Sir Cedric Hardwicke, Judith Anderson, and Cyril Ritchard.
Robert Montgomery Presents (hour), "Son of Adam" with Raymond Massey.

Studio One (hour), "A Favor for Sam" with James Whitmore.

TUESDAY
NBC: *Matinee Theater* (hour), "The Mating of Watkins Tottle" by Charles Dickens.
Armstrong Circle Theater (hour), "Man in Shadow" by David Padwa; alternates with *Playwrights '56.*

WEDNESDAY
NBC: *Matinee Theater* (hour), "Her Son's Wife" with Hope Lange.
Kraft Television Theater (hour), "The Fool Killer" adapted by Dale Wasserman from the novel by Helen Eustis.

THURSDAY
NBC: *Matinee Theater* (hour), "The Shining Palace" by Peggy Phillips.
Lux Video Theater (hour), "Criminal Code" by Martin Flavin.
CBS: *Climax* (hour), "The Louella Parsons Story" with Theresa Wright.
ABC: *Star Tonight* (½ hour), "Night Escape" by Abby Mann.

FRIDAY
NBC: *Matinee Theater* (hour), "The Odd Ones" by Betty Ulius.

SATURDAY
CBS: *Ford Star Jubilee* (1½ hours), "High Tor," a musical version of Maxwell Anderson's play with Bing Crosby, Julie Andrews, Everett Sloane, Nancy Olson, and Hans Conreid.

The 1957–58 and 1958–59 Seasons

1957–58

MONDAY
NBC: *Matinee Theater* (hour).
CBS: *Studio One* (hour).

TUESDAY
NBC: *Matinee Theater* (hour).

WEDNESDAY
  NBC: *Matinee Theater* (hour).
            Kraft Television Theater (hour).
  CBS: *U.S. Steel Hour* (hour); alternates with *Armstrong Circle Theater* (hour).

THURSDAY
  NBC: *Matinee Theater* (hour).

FRIDAY
  NBC: *Matinee Theater* (hour).

1958-59

WEDNESDAY
  CBS: *U.S. Steel Hour* (hour); alternates with *Armstrong Circle Theater* (hour).

THURSDAY
  CBS: *Playhouse 90* (1½ hours; often on tape).

Chapter Notes

Preface

1. Jack Gould, *New York Times,* March 8, 1955, p. 36.

Chapter 1

1. John Crosby, *Los Angeles Mirror,* November 1, 1960, II, p. 7.
2. NBC files, Remarks at a NBC Affiliates Meeting, October 23, 1960.
3. Hubbell Robinson, Jr., was interviewed twice by the author: in 1959 in a lengthy telephone conversation and in 1961 in Los Angeles. Robinson was quite eloquent; he spoke as well as he wrote.
4. Pat Weaver gave the author a three hour interview in 1959 in the manner of his brilliant and lengthy NBC memos (see Appendix I above).
5. *New York Times,* November 5, 1961, II, p. 19.
6. *Ibid.*
7. Hubbell Robinson, Jr., interview with the author, 1961.
8. Pat Weaver, interview with the author, 1959.
9. Giraud Chester and Garnet T. Garrison, *Television and Radio* (New York: Appleton, Century and Crofts, 1956), p. 59.
10. "Robert W. Sarnoff, an Interview," *Broadcasting,* September 8, 1957, p. 125.
11. *New York Times,* September 12, 1928, p. 1.
12. Orrin E. Dunlap, *The Outlook for Television* (New York: Harper and Brothers, 1932), p. 88.
13. Kenneth K. Jones, "A Survey of Television" (unpublished M.A. Thesis, Dept. of Theater Arts, Stanford University, 1949), p. 7.
14. In 1939 a far more light sensitive pickup tube was developed called the image orthicon tube. It replaced the iconoscope tube in the television camera.
15. Chester and Garrison, *op. cit.,* p. 42.

16. *The World Almanac and Book of Facts* (New York: World Telegram, 1939), p. 428.
17. *New York Times,* April 8, 1927, p. 1.
18. Richard Hubbell, *Television* (New York: Murray Hill Books, 1945), p. 97.
19. *New York Times,* April 27, 1931, p. 24.
20. "Television, 1939," a clipping folder, *Theatre Collection,* New York Public Library.
21. *Life,* June 20, 1938, pp. 22–23.
22. *New York Times,* June 12, 1938, X, p. 10.
23. "Television, 1938," a clipping folder, *Theatre Collection,* New York Public Library.
24. William C. Eddy, *Television, The Eyes of Tomorrow* (New York: Prentice-Hall, 1945), p. 4.
25. *New York Times,* May 22, 1938, XI, p. 10.
26. Thomas H. Hutchins, *Here Is Television* (New York: Hastings House, 1946), p. 158.
27. Orrin Dunlap, *New York Times,* September 3, 1939, IX, p. 8.
28. *New York Times,* July 23, 1939, p. 41; June 7, 1940, IX, p. 12.
29. Chester and Garrison, *op. cit.,* p. 42.
30. *Televiser,* November-December, 1945, p. 14. General Electric in Schenectady and DuMont in New York also tested television program service in this period.
31. Orrin E. Dunlap, *The Future of Television* (New York: Harper and Brothers, 1947), p. 186.
32. *New York Times,* July 6, 1941, X, p. 10.
33. *New York Times,* October 11, 1942, VIII, p. 10.
34. "What Happened to Television?" *Saturday Review,* February 21, 1942, p. 17.
35. Gilbert Seldes, *Saturday Review,* March 14, 1942, p. 13.
36. George Norford, interview with the author, 1958.

Chapter 2

1. *Broadcasting,* April 16, 1941, p. 13.
2. The growth of the networks was a natural and inevitable phenomenon. The idea was similar to the radio networks already in operation and they jumped right in. In addition, a new network was developed under the leadership of Dr. Allen B. DuMont. It ceased operation on September 15, 1955, although continuing to own a few stations. CBS and NBC record a growth to 1956 of 158 and 200 directly connected stations respectively (*Broadcasting Yearbook* [Washington: Broadcast Publications, 1958], pp. A-446, A-453). In those days NBC and CBS had large production facilities in contrast to ABC, which relied heavily on film and remote pick-ups. For example, CBS in 1956 had 29 broadcast studios:

22 in New York, 5 in Hollywood, and 2 in Chicago—a $28 million investment in program production facilities (U.S. Congress, Senate, *Part IV, Network Practices,* Hearings before the Committee on Interstate and Foreign Commerce [Washington: U.S. Gov. Printing Office, 1957], pp. 24–28).

3. *Letter from AT&T to NBC.* New York, AT&T, November, 1945, pp. 1–7. The alternate to the use of coaxial cable, which was an electrical interconnection between cities, was kinescoped film, or kinescopes, as they came to be called. Recordings of television programs were photographed from the face of a kinescope tube and shipped from city to city. The poor quality of the reproduced picture was a serious defect of this system.

4. *Broadcasting,* February 12, 1945, p. 70.

5. *New York Times,* June 13, 1947, p. 34.

6. *Broadcasting,* January 4, 1947, p. 15.

7. *Broadcasting,* May 20, 1947, p. 28. It was not until May, 1948 that the FCC provided a graduated scale allowing new stations to broadcast less in their early months of operation (*Broadcasting,* May 10, 1948, p. 22).

8. "What Happened to TV?" *Saturday Review,* February 21, 1942, pp. 15ff. When radio and talking pictures came along Hollywood had also tried to delay or prevent their growth for fear they would kill the industry.

9. On this one the filmmakers temporarily succeeded. In the early 1960s the film theater chains in California spearheaded a "Proposition 13" method to halt ex–NBC executive Pat Weaver's massive subscription television operation. Eventually the California Supreme Court reversed them. They waged a sick, reactionary campaign and slowed down Weaver's efforts until it became too late to save this pioneering attempt at pay television on cable.

10. Director-Producer Albert McCleery was very cooperative. He was extensively interviewed in New York in 1959 and again in 1961 in Los Angeles.

11. Philip Gustafson, "Nickelodeon Days of Television," *Nation's Business,* July 1947, p. 36.

12. *Follow-Up,* a CBS brochure, 1952.

13. In an interview with the author, Robert Lewine, publicity director at NBC in the late fifties, declared: "Drama was an obvious form. It was sort of a little theater club. It was easy to put on plays and there were many plays available at first. It was just a very easy form to do—back in 1945–46–47—for five or six thousand dollars. This was about all the medium could stand." Jack Gould in *The New York Times* commented, "video art is seriously deficient . . . the finished show frequently bears too close a resemblance to the uncertain efforts of a summer theatre apprentice group" (November 10, 1948, Sec. II, p. 9).

14. Much was written about Fred Coe by his stable of playwrights and he is relatively easy to document, which is just as well since he was very difficult to schedule for an interview. He did submit to several telephone interviews and was unusually accurate in remembering what happened.

(Researchers will verify that accounts vary considerably when different subjects look back several years on what happened.)

15. Fred Coe studied at the Yale School of Drama in 1938–40. He directed the Civic Theater in Columbia, South Carolina, for four years and in April, 1945, was hired as a production assistant by NBC. He directed the *Theatre Guild*, *ANTA* and *Kraft* shows and became the producer, as well as occasional director and writer, of the famed *Philco Television Playhouse*, the *Producer's Showcase* series, *Playwrights '56*, and in 1958–59, *Playhouse 90* for CBS (This compilation comes from a number of sources, including the *Dictionary of National Biography*, the NBC Files, and *The New York Times*).

16. *Televiser*, May, 1946, see front cover; and *Variety*, January 22, 1947, p. 31.

17. Bob Stahl, *Variety*, April 30, 1947, p. 36; Judy Dupuy, *Televiser*, May-June, 1947, p. 36.

18. *Kraft Television Theater*, NBC files.

19. *Television*, October, 1946, p. 12.

20. Edmund Rice, NBC files.

21. Bob Stahl, *Variety*, May 14, 1947, p. 38. The production was housed in a tiny studio on a side corridor in Radio City and broadcast to an audience of less than 40,000. There were only slightly more than 43,000 sets in the nation at this time—*Kraft Television Theater*, NBC files.

22. *Variety*, May 14, 1947, p. 38; *Televiser*, May-June, 1947, p. 36; and *Variety*, May 21, 1947, p. 42.

23. *Variety*, May 7, 1957, p. 50.

24. J. Walter Thompson Agency, "Television First," a company handout and company publicity files.

25. Edmund Rice, *Best Television Plays*, ed. by William I. Kaufman (New York: Merlin Press, 1950), Vol. I, p. 94.

26. Maury Holland, *ibid.*, pp. 3ff.

27. *Broadcasting*, March 8, 1948, p. 17; and *New York Times*, March 18, 1948, p. 54.

28. *Broadcasting*, April 5, 1947, p. 30; *ibid.*, April 12, 1948, p. 29.

29. *New York Times*, March 29, 1948, p. 48; *ibid.*, April 12, 1948, p. 40.

30. *Broadcasting*, February 16, 1948, p. 15.

31. *New York Times*, December 29, 1947, p. 27; *ibid.*, July 13, 1948, X, p. 1.

32. *Variety*, October 20, 1947, p. 1.

33. Joe Laurie, Jr., and Abel Green, *Show Biz, from Vaude to Video* (New York: Henry Holt, 1951), pp. 532ff.

34. Ben Gross, *I Looked and I Listened* (New York: Random House, 1954), p. 281.

35. *New York Times*, October 25, 1947, p. 30.

36. *Ibid.*, p. 19.

37. Bob Stahl, *Variety*, November 12, 1947, p. 34. It is true that the play has a mortgaged homestead, a villain, a ravished daughter and a brother who avenges her honor (St. John Ervine, "John Ferguson," *British and American Plays* [New York: Oxford Press, 1949], pp. 380–473).

38. Gould criticized the Guild for allowing sentiment to influence the choice of production, stating that Ervine was the "daddy of the soap-opera writers" (*New York Times*, November 16, 1947, II, p. 11).
39. *Variety*, April 7, 1948, p. 29.
40. *New York Times*, December 2, 1947, p. 58.
41. Chester and Garrison, *Television and Radio* (1950), *op. cit.*, p. 43.
42. *New York Times*, April 24, 1949, X, pp. 1–3; *ibid.*, January 1, 1950, II, p. 9.
43. Robert Nimmo, "An Analysis of Network Television Programming" (unpublished M.S. Thesis, Boston University, 1956), p. 22.
44. Nimmo, *op. cit.*, p. 19.
45. The Philco Corporation, Ford Motor Company and later dramatic series sponsors such as U.S. Steel, Hallmark Cards, and Lever Brothers (Lux Soap) all had previously sponsored drama on radio.
46. A result of this trend was the large number of masters' theses on television at this time which concerned themselves with the adaptation of stage plays to television. See the *Speech Monograph* and the *American Educational Theater Journal*.
47. *New York Times*, October 24, 1948, p. 11.
48. *Variety*, December 18, 1947, p. 41.
49. For example, Gould's comments on Philco's *Angel in the Wings*, in contrast to his praise of *Dinner at Eight*, and *Counsellor-at-Law* for their "fresh perspective" (*New York Times*, October 31, 1948, II, p. 11).
50. Jack Gould, *ibid.*, March 12, 1948, p. 46, and *Variety*, April 14, 1948, p. 26.
51. *Ibid.*, October, 1949, p. 29.
52. *Variety*, August 25, 1948, p. 11.
53. *Ibid.*, November 17, 1948, p. 28.
54. *New York Times*, May 26, 1949, p. 58.
55. *Variety*, June 14, 1950, p. 41.
56. *Time*, May, 1950, p. 63.
57. This biographical information is compiled from a number of sources, including the *Dictionary of National Biography*, *New York Times*, the NBC files and several interviews.
58. George Rosen, *Variety*, November 10, 1948, p. 35.
59. Worthington Miner, interview with the author, 1959.
60. Jack Gould, *New York Times*, February 15, 1949, p. 41.
61. *Variety*, March 9, 1949, p. 33.
62. Phillip Miller, *Consumer Reports*, April 1949, p. 187; Flora Schreiber, "Television, A New Idiom," *Hollywood Quarterly*, Winter, 1949, p. 184.
63. Miner interview.
64. Jack Gould, *New York Times*, October 26, 1950, p. 50. The pioneering nature of the settings designed by Don Gilman can be verified by comparing the floor plans with those of other productions in *The Best Television Plays of the Year* (New York: Merlin Press, 1950), pp. 5, 56, 80,

112, 137, 167, 193, 221, 254. There were approximately six or seven settings of the various places on the battleship: the bridge, quarters, control tower, turrets, etc. Cut-outs were used extensively and rear screen
projections provided backgrounds. Tilting platforms suggested the ship
was sinking and film clips and models were used to suggest the battle.

65. Maurice Valency, "Battleship Bismarck," *The Best Television Plays of the
Year,* ed. by William Kaufman (New York: Merlin Press, 1950), pp.
254–310.

66. *Ibid.,* pp. 252ff.

67. Miner interview.

68. *Ibid.*

69. Jack Gould, *New York Times,* October 24, 1951.

70. *Variety,* February 6, 1952, pp. 27, 41. Weaver's activities at this time went
under the title "Operation Frontal Lobe," and received considerable
ridicule in the press. Among these activities were NBC's first attempts
to get writers and actors under long term contract for the dramatic series
(*ibid.,* February 13, 1952, p. 29). *Variety* reported of Miner in 1952–53,
however, that he was "despairing of idleness" and was now trying to sell
shows to advertisers himself because NBC was not giving him work
(*Variety,* March 12, 1953, p. 33).

71. Rod Serling, *op. cit.,* p. 8.

72. Miner interview.

73. *Ibid.*

74. *Variety,* September 20, 1950, p. 31; Val Adams, *New York Times,*
September 30, 1950, p. 30; Jack Gould, *ibid.,* October 11, 1950, p. 66.

Chapter 3

1. *Variety,* September 29, 1948, p. 46.

2. "Chevrolet Tele-Theater," NBC files.

3. "Colgate Theater," NBC files.

4. *Variety,* July 13, 1949, p. 49.

5. *Ibid.,* and "Lights Out," NBC files.

6. Fred Coe, "Something in the Wind," *The Best Television Plays for the
Year,* ed. by William Kaufman (New York: Merlin Press, 1951), pp.
197–215.

7. "Lights Out," NBC files.

8. *Variety,* February 22, 1950, p. 29.

9. Jack Gould, *New York Times,* October 3, 1950, p. 63.

10. R.L. Shayon, *Saturday Review,* April 21, 1951, p. 31. Some other
Maugham novels which were dramatized were *Theatre, The Moon and
Sixpence,* and *Cakes and Ale.*

11. R.L. Shayon, *ibid.,* March 24, 1951, pp. 28ff.

12. R.L. Shayon, *ibid.,* October 28, 1950, p. 48 and November 18, 1950,
p. 34. Of the Robert Montgomery show Shayon caustically remarked,

"Even Academy Award winners turn out to be hardly more than stage-waits for the bouncy, bubbly, gay, delightful, sparking routine of the 'Be Happy Go Lucky' troupe of singers..."

13. Robert Lewine, interview with the author, 1958.
14. *New York Times,* October 7, 1950, p. 32.
15. Phillip Miller, *Consumer Reports,* April 1949, p. 187.
16. *Broadcasting,* April 25, 1949, p. 85. The Peabody Broadcasting Awards were established in 1940 to honor a benefactor of the University of Georgia, the late George Foster Peabody. They were jointly administered by the University of Georgia School of Journalism and the N.A.R.T.B.
17. *The Best Television Plays of the Year, 1950* (New York: Merlin Press, 1952), p. 78. Their premiere, however, was Tennessee Williams' *Portrait of a Madonna,* produced by Hume Cronyn and starring Jessica Tandy. It is a one-act mood piece about a mentally deranged Southern belle and Tandy was praised for a "powerful, poignant picture" in "a thirty minute monologue" (Bronson, *Variety,* September 29, 1948, p. 46).
18. *New York Times,* October 7, 1950, p. 32.
19. A producer, director and writer who came to prominence with his defense of live television drama in the late 1950s.
20. *Variety,* September 26, 1951, p. 23.
21. "Masterpiece Playhouse," NBC files.
22. *New York Times,* May 6, 1951, II, p. 9.
23. "Robert Montgomery Presents," NBC files.
24. Fred Coe, "Television Drama's Declaration of Independence," *Theatre Arts,* June, 1954, pp. 31–32, p. 80.

Chapter 4

1. *The World Almanac,* 1952, p. 506.
2. *New York Times,* April 14, 1952, p. 52.
3. *Broadcasting-Telecasting Yearbook, 1954–55* (Washington: Broadcasting-Telecasting, 1956), p. 15.
4. Chester and Garrison, *op. cit.,* p. 45.
5. Robert D. Swezy, "Give the TV Code a Chance," *Quarterly of Film, Radio and Television,* VII, Fall, 1952, p. 24.
6. *New York Times,* June 25, 1951, p. 1.
7. Green and Laurie, Jr., *op. cit.*
8. *Variety,* July 16, 1952, pp. 1, 57; and July 2, 1952, p. 24.
9. *New York Times,* November 23, 1952, II, p. 13.
10. Jack Gould, *ibid.*
11. *Ibid.*
12. The arguments about live *versus* filmed drama persisted from 1952–53 on, until filmed drama superseded live entirely. While he was decrying the film's first splurge as "the colossal boner of the year," Jack Gould

surveyed the arguments for live television drama: 1. The pictures on
film are "just plain bad." The visual and aural aspects of film lack that
"intangible sense of depth and trueness." 2. The films are most un-
satisfactory in terms of content; they are mostly "pedestrian little half-
hour quickies that are cluttering up the networks." 3. The vast majority
have little more panorama than the live shows produced in New
York. 4. The perfection of film is artificial and is achieved only at the
price of the reality and spontaneity that are "part and parcel of the 'live,'
continuous performance." 5. The lasting magic of television is that it
employs a mechanical means to achieve an unmechanical end. (Jack
Gould, *New York Times,* December 14, 1952, p. 13.)

13. *Variety,* October 10, 1951, p. 25; and July 11, 1951, p. 33.
14. *Ibid.,* October 10, 1951, p. 25.
15. Jack Gould, *New York Times,* December 23, 1951, II, p. 11.
16. *New York Times,* May 2, 1952, p. 27. The other was Actor's Studio.
17. *Variety,* April 9, 1952, p. 35. The Celanese revivals of past Broadway suc-
    cesses were quite distinguished. It premiered with Thomas Mitchell in
    Eugene O'Neill's *Oh Wilderness;* this was followed by S.N. Behrman's
    No Time for Comedy with Jean-Pierre Aumont and his *Brief Moment*
    with Veronica Lake; Elmer Rice's *Counsellor-at-Law* with Aldred Drake;
    Street Scene, Anna Christie, Reunion in Vienna, Saturday Children and
    so on.
18. *Variety,* October 10, 1951, p. 25.
19. *New York Times,* December 11, 1951, p. 51.
20. *Ibid.,* April 11, 1952, p. 38.
21. *Variety,* April 16, 1952, p. 27.
22. Rod Serling, *Patterns* (New York: Simon and Schuster, 1957), pp. 5ff.
23. *Ibid.,* p. 7.
24. *Ibid.,* p. 9.
25. Ring Lardner, Jr., "Television's New Realism," *The Nation,* August 13,
    1955, p. 131.
26. *New York Times,* October 8, 1951, p. 28.
27. *Variety,* September 23, 1953, p. 23.
28. Paddy Chayefsky, "Holiday Song," *Television Plays* (New York: Simon
    and Schuster, 1955), pp. 3–37.
29. *Variety,* September 23, 1952, p. 36.
30. Chayefsky, "Printer's Measure," *op. cit.,* pp. 43–81.
31. Chayefsky, "Marty," *op. cit.,* pp. 135–172.
32. Jack Gould, *New York Times,* May 25, 1953, p. 43.
33. "The Mother" was produced on Philco Television Playhouse in May, 1954.
34. Chayefsky, "Marty," *op. cit.,* pp. 173–4.
35. Chayefsky, "The Big Deal," *op. cit.,* pp. 91–125.
36. *Variety,* July 22, 1953, p. 31.
37. Quoted in *Saturday Review,* April 16, 1955, p. 13.
38. Horton Foote, "The Trip to Bountiful," *Harrison Texas* (New York: Har-
    court, Brace, 1956), pp. 189–218.

39. Foote, "A Young Lady of Property," *ibid.*, pp. 3–40.
40. The premiere was Robert Alan Aurthur's *Cafe Society*, with Rod Steiger as the camera's voice (*Variety*, July 18, 1953, p. 35).
41. Foote, "Tears of My Sister," *ibid.*, pp. 77–97.
42. Tad Mosel, "Ernie Barger Is Fifty," *Other People's Houses* (New York: Simon and Schuster, 1958), pp. 5–37.
43. *Variety*, August 12, 1953, p. 24.
44. Mosel, *op. cit.*, p. xi.
45. *Ibid.*, p. ix.
46. Edmund Rice, *Best Television Plays*, ed. by William J. Kaufman (New York: Merlin Press, 1950), I, p. 94; and interview with the author, 1959.
47. Mosel, *op. cit.*, pp. 115ff.
48. "Philco Television Playhouse," NBC files.
49. Rod Serling, *Patterns* (New York: Simon and Schuster, 1957), pp. 12–14.
50. Jack Gould, *New York Times*, February 2, 1953, p. 31.
51. Serling, *op. cit.*, pp. 14ff.
52. Jack Gould, *New York Times*, April 12, 1953, II, p. 11.
53. *Variety*, April 8, 1953, p. 25.
54. *New York Times*, January 31, 1954, II, p. 13.
55. Serling, *op. cit.*, pp. 183–240.
56. "Kraft Television Theater," NBC files.
57. Serling, *op. cit.*, p. 242.
58. *Ibid.*, p. 178.
59. *Ibid.*, pp. 179ff.
60. *Variety*, August 12, 1953, p. 24.
61. Serling, *op. cit.*, pp. 143–177.
62. "Edmund Rice," NBC files.
63. *Variety*, April 22, 1953, p. 23.
64. "Kraft Television Theater," NBC files.
65. "Television" clipping folder, New York Public Library Theater Collection.
66. Jack Gould, *New York Times*, May 13, 1953, p. 40.
67. George Norford, who was publicity director for NBC in these years, mentioned *Hamlet* in an interview as among great network achievements. Also "Hallmark Hall of Fame," NBC files.
68. *Time*, May 2, 1953, p. 59.
69. Jack Gould, *New York Times*, April 27, 1953, p. 29.
70. Flora Schreibner, "Television's *Hamlet*," *Quarterly of Film, Radio and Television*, Winter, 1953, Vol. VIII, No. 2, p. 150.
71. R.L. Shayon, *Saturday Review*, May 16, 1953, p. 33.
72. Maurice Evans, "Hallmark Hall of Fame," NBC files.
73. *Ibid.*
74. *New York Times*, April 27, 1953, p. 29.
75. Albert McCleery, interview with the author, 1961.
76. *Variety*, April 8, 1953, p. 26.
77. McCleery interview.
78. *New York Times*, November 4, 1952, p. 1.

79. *Ibid.,* December 17, 1952, p. 29.
80. Val Adams, *New York Times,* September 22, 1954, p. 40.
81. R.L. Shayon, *Saturday Review,* January 16, 1954, p. 34.
82. George Rosen, *Variety,* September 22, 1954, p. 29. An attempt has been made to locate these two dramas but they were not in the NBC files or the New York Public Library and no one remembered them.
83. *New York Times,* February 18, 1955, p. 28.
84. *Variety,* October 29, 1952, p. 33.
85. Jack Gould, *New York Times,* December 5, 1952, p. 42.
86. George Rosen, *Variety,* December 3, 1952, p. 24.

Chapter 5

1. *Variety,* September 30, 1953, p. 27. Perhaps the biggest headlines and the widest use of television occurred during the Army-McCarthy hearings from April to June of that season.
2. *Broadcasting-Telecasting,* January 11, 1954, p. 89.
3. Television's "follow-the-leader" program cycles are described often throughout. Television is no more notorious in this respect than any of the mass media but since it quickly became "the" mass media it also receives more criticism for this kind of programming.
4. *New York Times,* September 7, 1955, p. 63.
5. Chester and Garrison, *op. cit.,* p. 48. The color controversy is ably chronicled by Kenneth R. Jones, *op. cit.,* pp. 55–65.
6. *Broadcasting-Telecasting,* December 21, 1953, p. 21.
7. Chester and Garrison, *op. cit.,* p. 49.
8. *Broadcasting-Telecasting Yearbook, 1954-55, op. cit.,* p. 15.
9. *Broadcasting-Telecasting Yearbook 1955-56, op. cit.,* p. 15.
10. "Sylvester L. 'Pat' Weaver," NBC files.
11. Pat Weaver, "Opportunities in Television," *Variety,* January 16, 1952, pp. 25, 38.
12. *Variety,* February 6, 1952, p. 27.
13. *Variety,* October 1, 1954, p. 1.
14. Max Liebman, "Variety and Television," *Television in the Making,* ed. by Paul Rothan (New York: Hastings House, 1956), p. 77.
15. Jack Gould, *New York Times,* September 15, 1954, p. 44.
16. *Broadcasting-Telecasting,* September 20, 1954, p. 16.
17. John Crosby, *New York Herald Tribune,* September 15, 1954, p. 30.
18. Jack Gould, *New York Times,* September 26, 1954, p. 44.
19. *Variety,* October 1, 1954, p. 1.
20. *New York Times,* October 21, 1954, p. 39.
21. *Variety,* October 21, 1954, p. 23.
22. *Ibid.,* November 3, 1954, p. 31.
23. *Ibid.,* February 2, 1955, p. 33.
24. *Broadcasting-Telecasting Yearbook, 1955-56, op. cit.,* p. 32.

25. Robert Lewine, interview with the author, 1958.
26. Pat Weaver, interview with the author, 1959.
27. *Ibid.*
28. *Ibid.*
29. See Chapter VIII, when CBS under the creative leadership of Hubbell Robinson, Jr., produces the Playhouse 90 series *et al.*
30. *New York Times*, December 20, 1954, p. 29.
31. Pat Weaver, *Variety*, October 13, 1954, p. 29.
32. *Ibid.*
33. Max Liebman, *op. cit.*, p. 77.
34. Weaver interview, 1959.
35. Lester Bernstein, interview with the author, 1958; and "'Television's Lords of Creation," *Harpers*, November, 1956, and December, 1956.
36. George Rosen, *Variety*, October 20, 1954, p. 25.
37. Jack Gould, *New York Times*, November 17, 1954, p. 45.
38. James M. Barrie, *Peter Pan* (New York: Scribner's, 1950), pp. 3–162.
39. Jack Gould, *New York Times*, March 8, 1955, p. 33.
40. George Rosen, *Variety*, March 9, 1955, p. 33.
41. Weaver interview.
42. *Ibid.*

Chapter 6

1. *New York Times*, April 15, 1954, p. 43.
2. "Philco Television Playhouse," NBC files.
3. *Variety*, September 2, 1953, p. 26.
4. Tad Mosel, *op. cit.*, p. 38.
5. Mosel, *Other People's Houses, ibid.*, pp. 40–73.
6. Mosel, "The Haven," *ibid.*, pp. 77–113.
7. *Ibid.*, p. 75.
8. Serling, *op. cit.*, p. 19.
9. *Variety*, October 14, 1953, p. 34.
10. Chayefsky, *op. cit.*, pp. 259–263.
11. Patricia O'Connor, "An Analysis of Selected Original Television Dramas" (Unpublished M.A. thesis, Department of Speech and Drama, Catholic University of America, 1958), p. 53.
12. Chayefsky, *op. cit.*, p. 178.
13. Chayefsky, "The Mother," *op. cit.*, pp. 183–218. *Variety* said of this play: "Paddy Chayefsky is undoubtedly one of the outstanding writing talents in the television business today, and he proved it again with a bang" (April 7, 1954, p. 36).
14. Gore Vidal (ed.), "Best Television Plays of the Year," *op. cit.*, p. 220.
15. Gilbert Seldes wrote in November of 1955: "This predilection for the 'down beat' or sad ending got Mr. Coe into trouble last season, but these

writers are still writing the kind of television plays which have this special quality." (Gilbert Seldes, *New York Times,* November 28, 1955, VI, p. 55.)

16. J.P. Miller, "The Rabbit Trap," *Best Television Plays of the Year, op. cit.,* pp. 191–220.
17. *Variety,* December 1, 1954, p. 27.
18. Robert Alan Aurthur, "Man on a Mountain Top," *Best Television Plays of the Year, op. cit.,* pp. 110–134.
19. Gore Vidal, *Visit to a Small Planet* (Boston: Little, Brown, 1956), pp. 221–248.
20. Vidal, *op. cit.,* p. 170.
21. *Variety,* May 17, 1950, p. 27.
22. Paddy Chayefsky, "Good Theatre in Television," *How to Write for Television,* ed. by William I. Kaufman (New York: Hastings House, 1955), p. 44.
23. Chayefsky, *op. cit.,* p. xi.
24. *Ibid.,* p. xii.
25. Horton Foote, *Variety,* May 23, 1956, p. 31.
26. Vincent Donehue, *Variety,* May 23, 1956, p. 31.
27. Delbert Mann, *ibid.,* p. 32.
28. Mosel, *op. cit.,* p. 74.

Chapter 7

1. George Rosen, *Variety,* October 24, 1953, p. 33.
2. Edmund Rice, NBC files.
3. *Ibid.*
4. *New York Times,* June 10, 1955, p. 45.
5. Edmund Rice, interview with the author, 1959.
6. Jack Gould, *New York Times,* May 7, 1954, p. 33.
7. "Kraft Television Theater," NBC files.
8. *Variety,* June 16, 1954, p. 23.
9. *New York Times,* January 20, 1954, p. 30.
10. *Ibid.,* November 30, 1955, p. 67.
11. Rod Serling, *op. cit.,* pp. 84ff.
12. *Ibid.,* pp. 48–85.
13. Jack Gould, *New York Times,* January 17, 1955, p. 45.
14. *Time,* February 9, 1955, p. 60.
15. Robert Chandler, *Variety,* February 16, 1955, p. 34.
16. John Crosby, *New York Herald Tribune,* February 9, 1955.
17. Ben Radim, "A Seacoast in Bohemia," *The Best Television Plays,* ed. by William I. Kaufman (New York: Merlin Press, 1954), (Vol. III), pp. 9–55.
18. Dale Wasserman and Jack Balch, "Elisha and the Long Knives," *Top*

Television Shows of the Year, 1954-55, ed. by Irving Settel (New York: Hastings House, 1955), p. 30.

19. "The revival was distressingly inept"—"An exercise in frenzy" (Jack Gould, *New York Times,* February 25, 1955, p. 28). "It didn't come off with continuity and impact" (Robert Chandler, *Variety,* March 2, 1955, p. 30).
20. *Variety,* March 2, 1955, p. 25.
21. *Ibid.,* April 13, 1955, p. 32.
22. *Ibid.,* September 30, 1953, p. 27.
23. *New York Times,* January 10, 1954, II, p. 5.
24. *Variety,* August 12, 1953, p. 23.
25. Bob Hull, *Los Angeles Herald Examiner,* October 21, 1964, A-17.
26. Albert McCleery, interview with the author, 1959.
27. Jack Gould, *New York Times,* January 27, 1954, p. 25. John Crosby in *The Herald Tribune* agreed with Gould but George Rosen in *Variety* described it as a triumph for all . . . with the major laurels going to the production. . . (John Crosby, *New York Herald Tribune,* January 29, 1954, p. 48; and George Rosen, *Variety,* January 27, 1954, p. 37.)
28. McCleery interview.
29. *Ibid.*
30. Maurice Evans, "Hallmark Hall of Fame," NBC files.
31. McCleery interview; *Variety,* May 19, 1954, p. 33.
32. "Hallmark Hall of Fame," NBC files.
33. *Newsweek,* December 13, 1954, p. 62; *Broadcasting-Telecasting,* December 16, 1954, p. 14; and *New York Times,* November 29, 1954, p. 32.
34. Jack Gould, *New York Times,* September 23, 1953, p. 44 and December 13, 1953, II, p. 19; Robert Chandler, *Variety,* September 23, 1953, p. 33.
35. Gore Vidal (ed.), *Best Television Plays* (New York: Ballantine Books, Inc., 1956), p. 68.
36. Reginald Rose, "Thunder on Sycamore Street," *Six Television Plays* (New York: Simon and Schuster, 1947), pp. 59–104.
37. Rose, *op. cit.,* pp. 107ff.
38. *Ibid.,* p. 109.
39. *Variety,* April 13, 1955, p. 32.
40. *Variety,* December 1, 1954, p. 27.
41. Rose, *op. cit.,* pp. 155ff.
42. Rose, "12 Angry Men," *op. cit.,* pp. 113–153.
43. Leonard Traube, *Variety,* September 22, 1954, p. 31. A second "superior dramatic work" by Rose was *An Almanac of Liberty,* suggested by a book by Supreme Court Justice William O. Douglas. *Broadcasting-Telecasting* felt that "Mr. Douglas' treatment was academic" in comparison to the television play, and Rose himself regards it as "one of the few dramas that might be classified as 'controversial' which has appeared on a national television show. . ." (*Broadcasting-Telecasting,* November 15, 1954, p. 14; Rose, "An Almanac of Liberty," *op. cit.,* p. 206).

44. Rose, *op. cit.*, p. xii.
45. U.S. Congress, Senate, *Part IV, Network Practices, Hearings before the Committee on Interstate and Foreign Commerce* (Washington, D.C.: U.S. Gov. Printing Office, 1957), pp. 1736–1752.
46. New York Times, November 14, 1954, II, p. 11.
47. Leonard Traube, *Variety*, October 13, 1954, p. 31; Jack Gould, *New York Times*, April 25, 1955, p. 30; *ibid.*, July 29, 1955, p. 35; Gould, *ibid.*, November 14, 1954, II, p. 11; *ibid.*, May 27, 1955, p. 36.
48. *Variety*, July 6, 1955, p. 28; *Broadcasting-Telecasting*, October 10, 1955, p. 40.
49. "...[O]ne of the season's notable achievements, a vigorous yet sensitive insight into the repair of the minds of troubled G.I.'s who were subjected to Commie 'brain washing.' Superbly directed and beautifully played, it was topical theatre of both pertinency and power" (Jack Gould, *New York Times*, October 25, 1953, p. 13).
50. *Variety*, October 25, 1953, p. 36.
51. *Newsweek*, November 11, 1953, p. 70.
52. *Broadcasting-Telecasting Yearbook, 1955-56, op. cit.; Look*, December 28, 1954, p. 101.
53. Jack Gould, *New York Times*, April 4, 1954, Sec. II, p. 13; *Variety*, April 7, 1954, p. 29.
54. Gould, *New York Times*, January 10, 1954, II, p. 15.
55. Statement by Ellen Heagerty, ABC personnel relations, in an interview with the author, 1958. Heagerty explained that the American Broadcasting Company maintained "no records of its achievements."
56. *New York Times*, January 3, 1954, Sec. II, p. 11 and May 21, 1954, p. 23.
57. Rose Serling, "The Rack," *op. cit.*, pp. 99–138.
58. *Ibid.*
59. Jack Gould, *New York Times*, March 18, 1955, p. 39.
60. Rose, *op. cit.*, p. 253.
61. *Ibid.*, pp. 253ff.
62. Jack Gould, *New York Times*, August 7, 1955, II, p. 11.
63. *Variety*, July 20, 1955, pp. 27, 36.

Chapter 8

1. Robert W. Sarnoff, "Letter to Radio-Television Editors," August 22, 1957, NBC files.
2. Sarnoff, "Address at the NBC Affiliates Meeting" (New York: October 23, 1958).
3. *Broadcasting-Telecasting*, November 19, 1951, p. 13.
4. *New York Times*, April 2, 1957, p. 69.
5. Hal Humphry, *Los Angeles Mirror*, circa 1960. This writer collected Humphry's columns for his personal file and many are not annotated.

6. *Ibid.*, July 1, 1961, p. 9.
7. Huber Ellingsworth, "Entertainment Radio in the 1950s: More Than Afterglow of the Golden Age," Edward Jay Whetmore, *Mediamerica* (Belmont, Calif.: Wadsworth Publishing, 1987), p. 103.
8. *New York Times,* October 28, 1956, II, p. 13.
9. See the *New York Times* program schedules from September, 1956 to February, 1957.
10. *New York Times,* October 28, 1956, II, p. 13.
11. *Ibid.; Broadcasting-Telecasting,* August 13, 1956, p. 38.
12. *Variety,* February 20, 1957, p. 21.
13. *Broadcasting-Telecasting,* April 15, 1957, p. 31.
14. Robert Austin Smith, "Television: The Light That Failed," *Fortune,* December, 1958, p. 161.
15. Robert W. Sarnoff, "Letter to Radio-Television Editors," December 2, 1957, NBC files.
16. Florence Britton, ed., *Best Television Plays, 1957* (New York: Ballentine Books, 1957), p. 7.
17. *Broadcasting-Telecasting,* December 30, 1957, pp. 68, 70.
18. Robert W. Lewine, "Television's New Generation," an address, Ithaca, New York, October 11, 1958, NBC files.
19. *New York Times,* October 5, 1956, p. 53.
20. Hubbell Robinson, Jr., interview with the author, 1961.
21. *Ibid.*
22. Jack Gould, *New York Times,* March 10, 1957, Sec. II, p. 11.
23. *New York Times,* December 7, 1957, p. 55.
24. Serling, "Requiem for a Heavyweight," *op. cit.,* pp. 181–240.
25. Leonard Spinrad, interview with the author, 1958.
26. Lester Bernstein, interview with the author, 1958.
27. *Variety,* December 4, 1957, p. 29.
28. Robinson interview.
29. Albert McCleery, interview with the author, 1961.
30. Robinson, personal interview.
31. McCleery, personal interview.
32. Jane Murray, personal notes circa 1960 given to the author.
33. McCleery interview.
34. Jane Murray, interview with the author, 1961.
35. *Ibid.*
36. McCleery interview.
37. Jack Gould, *New York Times,* May 21, 1958, p. 67.
38. McCleery interview.

Chapter 9

1. *Variety,* October 12, 1955, p. 38.
2. *Ibid.,* December 21, 1955, p. 19.

3. The Fund for the Republic, for example, offered that season $20,000 to Armstrong Circle Theater's *I Was Accused* and $20,000 to Alcoa Hour's *Tragedy in a Temporary Town.* In each case the prize money was divided among the producer, director and writer (*New York Times,* July 22, 1956, p. 37).

4. "Kraft Television Theater," NBC files.

5. "Edmund Rice," NBC files.

6. Florence Britton, ed., *op. cit.,* p. 68.

7. William Noble, "Snapfinger Creek," *Best Television Plays, op. cit.,* pp. 69–98.

8. Edmund Rice, interview with the author, 1959.

9. John Crosby, *New York Herald Tribune,* April 2, 1956, p. 56.

10. Jack Gould, *New York Times,* March 29, 1956, p. 55.

11. *Variety,* April 4, 1956, p. 29.

12. Rice interview; NBC files.

13. Two other plays that Britton cited that season were *Even the Weariest River* by Alvin Sapinsley on the Alcoa Hour and *The Boarding House* by Will Lorin on the U.S. Steel Hour (Florence Britton, editor, *op. cit.,* pp. 222ff.)

14. Rice interview.

15. "Kraft Television Theater," NBC files.

16. *New York Times,* April 17, 1958, p. 63; May 25, 1958, II, p. 11.

17. Jack Gould, *New York Times,* April 27, 1958, II, p. 11.

18. "Kraft Television Theater," NBC files.

19. *Newsweek,* June 29, 1957, p. 82.

20. "Playwrights '56," NBC files.

21. Albert McCleery, interview with the author, 1961.

22. Fred Coe, interview with the author, 1958; "Playwrights '56," NBC files.

23. Rice interview.

24. Coe interview; NBC files.

25. Ted Mosel, "The Waiting Place," *op. cit.,* pp. 203–242.

26. *Variety,* December 22, 1955, p. 28.

27. Jack Gould, *New York Times,* September 20, 1955, p. 62.

28. *New York Times,* January 10, 1956, p. 63.

29. *Variety,* December 21, 1955, p. 19.

30. *New York Times,* April 12, 1956, p. 63.

31. "Hallmark Hall of Fame," NBC files.

32. *New York Times,* May 7, 1956, p. 53.

33. Gould, *New York Times,* May 22, 1955, p. 13.

34. *Variety,* January 18, 1956, p. 33; *New York Times,* March 12, 1956; *ibid.,* May 7, 1956, p. 53.

35. *Ibid.,* November 21, 1955, p. 55.

36. George Rosen, *Variety,* November 23, 1955, p. 34.

37. *Ibid.,* January 18, 1956, p. 33.

38. *New York Times,* November 10, 1956, p. 63.

39. Worthington Miner, interview with the author, 1959.

40. *Ibid.*
41. *Variety,* January 23, 1957, p. 36.
42. "Alcoa-Goodyear Hour," NBC files.
43. Martin Luray, "As the Life Goes Out of the Show," *New Republic,* September 16, 1957, p. 22.
44. *New York Times,* January 26, 1958, II, p. 13.
45. Jack Gould, *ibid.,* October 18, 1957, p. 49.
46. *Ibid.,* April 2, 1958, p. 63.
47. *Ibid.,* March 5, 1957, p. 62.
48. *Variety,* March 5, 1957, p. 1.
49. Jack Gould, *New York Times,* March 10, 1957, II, p. 11.
50. Miner interview.
51. Edmund Rice, interview with the author, 1959.
52. Albert McCleery, interview with the author, 1961.
53. "Fred Coe," NBC files.
54. Hubbell Robinson, Jr., "You, the Public Are to Blame!" *Los Angeles Times,* television guide, June 6, 1961, p. 14.
55. John Crosby, *Los Angeles Mirror,* November 1, 1960, II, p. 7.
56. *Ibid.,* September 21, 1961, p. 8.

Index

172 Index